D0663780

Disrupting Unemployment

David Nordfors, i4j co-chair, co-founder, editor-in-chief
Vint Cerf, i4j co-chair, co-founder
Max Senges, managing editor

The production of this book was made possible by a grant from the Ewing Marion Kauffman Foundation. The contents of this publication are solely the responsibility of i4j.

Copyright © 2016 by IIIJ Foundation

All rights reserved. This book may not be used or reproduced for sale, in whole or in part, including illustrations, without written permission from the publisher, except in the case of cited brief quotations embodied in critical articles and reviews.

Published by Ewing Marion Kauffman Foundation
4801 Rockhill Road
Kansas City, Missouri 64110

TABLE OF CONTENTS:

FOREWORD

The sinister notion that machines will someday kill all jobs has been around for at least 200 years. Yes, machines can replace people at work or change the work that is needed, and they always have. At the same time, the labor force participation in the world has remained quite stable for many generations, and on the whole, the middle class has been growing worldwide. Innovation can both kill and create work. i4j—Innovation for Jobs—is a leadership forum discussing how to disrupt unemployment and eradicate joblessness.

All people can create value—but for that to happen, we need to develop a people-centered, rather than a task-centered, economy. Today, we are very far from that. According to Gallup, of the five billion people on this planet aged fifteen or older, three billion work in some way. Most of them want full-time jobs, but only 1.3 billion have them. Of these, only 13 percent are fully engaged in their work, giving and receiving its full value.

This terrible waste of human capacity and mismanagement of people's desire to create value for each other is more than just very bad business. It is an insult to ourselves and to all human beings. We believe there are ways to move beyond the habit of rejecting and mistreating ourselves in this way.

The good news is that this is an epic opportunity for entrepreneurs. Soon, virtually everyone will have a smartphone, allowing innovations for the first time to compete for the value-creating capacity of people everywhere, around the clock. We can begin to focus on raising the value of people, rather than only lowering the cost of tasks.

All people can be offered jobs that are tailored to match their unique sets of skills, talents, and passions with the most valuable opportunities. People need jobs to raise families. Gigs are too unpredictable. Innovators can find new ways of satisfying the need for jobs—it does not have to be employment.

We invite you to be an active stakeholder in the innovation-for-jobs ecosystem, or at least take part in the discussion around it.

We can't yet say what the ecosystem that will disrupt unemployment will look like. There are still many choices in framing the "work" market, and just as many choices for the policies, financial indicators, macroeconomics, and business models that can influence this framework. For the present, finding the right questions may be even more important than answering them.

Coinciding with the release of this book, i4j will be convening, for the first time, stakeholders in the innovation-for-jobs ecosystem to talk shop at the i4j ECO Summit, kicking off in Silicon Valley, in January 2016. There, we will continue the search for both questions and answers.

We hope you enjoy the eclectic swarm of ideas in this first book of the Innovation for Jobs i4j Leadership Forum.

David Nordfors
Co-Chair, Co-Founder i4j
Editor-in-Chief

Vint Cerf
Co-Chair, Co-Founder i4j

Max Senges
Managing Editor

i4j VISIONS

Toward an Innovation-for-Jobs Economy

By Vint Cerf and David Nordfors, on behalf of the i4j Leadership Forum[1]

Aspects of the vision: How can innovation disrupt unemployment and create meaningful work for everyone? How can we create a strong middle class innovation economy? Imagine if innovative entrepreneurs could use technology to create jobs tailored to fit every person in the same way products and services can be tailored to match consumer tastes. What if this technology could match the innate abilities and passions of every individual with appropriate opportunities in a long-tail economy? Increasing the workforce to 100 percent of the population—with everyone doing things they like—could multiply the value of the workforce several times, transforming the economy. What might such an innovation economy look like? How could business, policy, and education leaders work together to make it happen?

About i4j Visions

This collection presents some i4j visions. It is neither absolute nor complete. It is an incomplete selection of good ideas shared among i4j thought leaders, either at our meetings or in our extremely active online discussion group.

---

1 Vint Cerf and David Nordfors are the co-chairs of the i4j Leadership Forum.

1

It is not possible to construct a full i4j vision without participating actively in the prolonged, lively, and informal discussion among the eclectic mix of imaginative people who agree and disagree in friendly, constructive ways. Much of the deeper understanding appears when good ideas that do not match are juxtaposed.

The vision presented here is merely a two-dimensional snapshot of a moving hologram constructed from a multitude of different perspectives. Consider it a tour guide to the i4j innovation for jobs ecosystem that is beginning to take shape.

The members of the i4j Leadership Forum have taken part in this effort by commenting and providing references for this text.

We are deeply grateful to our wordsmith, Alan Anderson, who has sought to weave many new ideas into a new, compelling narrative.

A New Narrative for Disrupting Unemployment

To address issues of work, employment, and unemployment, the IIIJ Foundation kicked off the i4j Summit on Innovation for Jobs with global thought leaders in March 2013.[2] At a time when the mainstream discussion was dominated by how technology might be taking away our jobs, i4j started a discussion about how innovation can instead "disrupt unemployment" and eradicate joblessness.[3] We are convinced that technology can be a force to enhance the value of people instead of diminishing their opportunities through automation.

This vocabulary is based on three assumptions: (1) all people can create value for each other; (2) the majority of human capacity— including those who are formally employed and those who are not—remains an untapped resource; and (3) an innovative and

---

2   For information about the 2013 i4j International Summit on Innovation for Jobs, see http://i4j.info/i4j/menlo-park-2013/. For white papers from the Summit, see http://i4j.info/i4j/menlo-park-2013/white-papers/.
3   David Nordfors, Sven Otto Littorin, and Anders Flodström, "Innovation AND Jobs—They're Not Mutually Exclusive," *Exconomy*, September 26, 2012, http://www.xconomy.com/san-francisco/2012/09/26/innovation-and-jobs/.

"disruptive" jobs strategy can liberate, compensate, and celebrate that resource. Underlying this vocabulary is our conviction that a job—which we broadly define as a regular activity that is rewarding both to the job-holder and to society—is a fundamental need.

Re-defining "Job" as a Need

In our vocabulary, a job is not merely a synonym for employment. When people say, "I need a job," they are making a very important statement that includes employment but also transcends it. They need a sustainable way of creating value that brings them the stability they need to support themselves and their families, yes; but they need more than this. They need a way of finding and tapping into their own unique talents, and of bringing those talents to others in ways that create value. Innovation for jobs is an effort to create more and better ways of expressing such needs to strengthen the individual, the community, and the economy.

The innovation for jobs narrative is enabled partly by the smartphone revolution, which heralded a new era of the world economy. Within just a few years, all people on the planet will be able to reach out to and engage with others in any geographical location, in real time. Imagine innovative entrepreneurs using technology to create jobs tailored to fit each person, just as products and services are designed to match the tastes of particular consumers. The Internet economy is, after all, user-centric. It is about personalization on a mass scale. A job is a need. The customer is the person who needs a good job. This document is an early step in the great adventure to discover who will serve the customer.

A People-Centered Economy

In a task-centered economy that seeks to minimize the cost of tasks, machines replace people as soon as the work can be automated. Things get cheaper to make. But people need to earn in order to spend, so the economy shrinks when the workforce shrinks. This is the present dilemma.

A people-centered economy that seeks to maximize the value of people, on the other hand, does not have that problem.[4] It is similar to replacing the mindsets from the present economy, which is designed around solving problems of scarcity, with an economy of abundance, which is designed around addressing an abundance of opportunities.[5]

Seen this way, the same technologies that people fear as job-killers can be used to match people and opportunities in creative new ways. Imagine an innovation ecosystem for jobs, with innovative companies competing to match the innate abilities and passions of each individual with the most valuable opportunities in a long-tail economy. A person in Damascus or Tel Aviv can team up with a person in Kansas City to serve a customer in Hong Kong. The traditional labor markets cannot do that, because they are designed to fill slots in production machines, not to optimize the value, abilities, and well-being of the global workforce. This type of matching is for the first time becoming possible with some of the freelance platforms that are emerging on the Internet.

The potential market for a better matching between people and opportunities is huge. Of the seven billion people in the world in 2011, five billion were aged fifteen or older. Gallup's chairman Jim Clifton says that three billion of them want to work. Most of them need full-time jobs, but there were only 1.2 billion "good jobs"[6] in the world.[7] According to Gallup's 2013 State of the Global Workplace Report,[8] only 13 percent of workers were engaged in their jobs, working with passion and feeling a profound connection to their company. Of the remaining 87 percent, 63 percent were "not

4   David Nordfors, "The Untapped $140 Trillion Innovation for Jobs Market," *TechCrunch*, February 21, 2015, http://techcrunch.com/2015/02/21/the-untapped-140-trillion-innovation-for-jobs-market/.

5   Jordan Greenhall, "The Coming Great Transition," *Medium*, November 24, 2014, https://medium.com/emergent-culture/the-coming-great-transition-e50d62da77d4#.vwogg55qk.

6   Gallup defines a "good job" as a formal employment offering steady work averaging 30 or more hours per week and a regular paycheck.

7   Jim Clifton, "The Coming Jobs War," *Gallup Business Journal*, September 7, 2011, http://www.gallup.com/businessjournal/149144/coming-jobs-war.aspx.

8   State of the Global Workplace Report 2013, Gallup. http://www.gallup.com/poll/165269/worldwide-employees-engaged-work.aspx.

engaged," lacking motivation. Outnumbering the engaged workers by nearly two to one, 24 percent were "actively disengaged," openly showing unhappiness with work. This undermines the work of others in their companies. On planet earth, jobs are much more often a source of frustration than fulfillment.

In other words, there are billions of customers craving good jobs. This is an opportunity to create an entrepreneurial innovation for jobs ecosystem. There is no lack of tasks and opportunities in the world. With an economy that focuses on maximizing the value of people, important tasks and good jobs may compete for people, instead of people competing for jobs.

What is the potential size of the innovation for jobs market? Applied to the entire world population, this scenario can multiply value creation in the world economy several times over, because teams of passionate people inspiring each other and doing what they are best at create so much more value than the same people are doing in typical work environments of today. It is a sizeable innovation for jobs market, waiting to happen.

In 2015, the i4j Leadership Forum came to the conclusion that the time has come to move from thought to action and to try to bootstrap the innovation for jobs ecosystem, beginning in Silicon Valley. The first meeting with interested contributors was set for January 28–29, 2016, the launch of the i4j ECO Summit and the planned release date of this book.

Of course, disrupting unemployment is complex, and will require all the synergies digital technologies can create. What might an innovation for jobs economy look like? What will it take for business, policy, and education leaders jointly to make it happen? This is what the i4j Leadership Forum is discussing.

i4j thought leaders have begun with several key ideas. First, the problem is not too much automation or innovation; the problem is that we are trying to run the new economy in the old way. The old way is about sitting for years in the same mental and physical cubicles where we perform standardized tasks and follow unchanging work manuals. In the new way we envision, tedious, non-rewarding habits are shed to make way for long-hidden truths: ~~all people have talent, and they can use that talent to create value.~~

Considering how to disrupt employment brings us to the challenge of replacing old institutions that have long been seen as the pillars of modern middle-class economies. It is difficult to release the full potential of people in traditional workplaces, as Katz Kiely observes: "~~Employers expect employees to wear a cloak of the 'professional persona' ... To share knowledge to help colleagues is often regarded as disruptive behavior: and thus a massive chunk of skills, knowledge, and experience are kept locked away to avoid upsetting the status quo~~ ..."[9] She points at the great opportunity offered by combining psychology, neuroscience, and social sciences with data science to identify how to drive action and induce behavior change. This can empower innovation for jobs ecosystems to disrupt not only the labor market, but also the mindset of what is considered work.

One question is how governments can keep up with the changing jobs market. Private firms will want to apply behavior-changing tools, and they have the resources and incentives to do so. But policymakers and the public sector cannot so easily change entrenched power structures and political customs. Fortunately, there are effective models to follow, such as the Small Business Innovation Research program in the United States, in which federal agencies set aside a small percentage of their budgets to invest in emerging, fast-growing private firms. As departments of labor and other branches of government observe the forces pressing society toward innovation for jobs, it becomes more likely that they will find their own ways to adapt and support the underlying technology.

---

9 Katz Kiely, "Innovation and Economics," *Innovation in Australia*, August 26, 2015, http://australianinnovation.blogspot.co.uk/2015/08/innovaton-and-economics.html.

The Old Job Market

The old model for hiring, promoting, and informing employees has many drawbacks. Most entrenched firms can be described as monocultures, resembling the large industrial farms that grow enormous amounts of a single crop. Firms have also developed the habit of "productizing" humans to fit the job markets. Job markets favor malleable workers who are uniform in their skills and reasons for working. Each person who works is viewed as interchangeable labor—a name and a number.

The rationale for creating such institutions is their scalable efficiency. We have implemented scalable efficiency by tightly specifying all activities and standardizing them so they are performed in the same efficient way anywhere in the organization.

The story of scalable efficiency is as old as the industrial age. As infrastructures and technology improved, companies grew larger to take advantage of the benefits of scale. They produced at greater volume to decrease costs and to improve margins. To coordinate the efforts of larger groups of people to service larger markets, companies created command-and-control hierarchies, people-and-process silos, and procedures that bring consistency and predictability.

Today, the industrial-age mindset stands in the way of fully realizing the promise of the digital revolution. Richard Straub writes that "'heroic' management actions, such as cutting jobs and investment as a response to currency fluctuations and their accounting impact on EPS, are applauded by stock markets, despite the damage to the longer-term value-creating capacity of the enterprise."[10] Straub observes that the focus on shareholder value is a "downgrading of the human being to a resource that can be sacrificed to short-term interests of shareholders and those who are supposed to exercise the stewardship of what Peter Drucker

---

10 Richard Straub, "The Human Difference," *Drucker Society Europe Blog*, March 24, 2015, http://www.druckerforum.org/blog/?p=802.

called the constitutive elements of modern society—our organizations and institutions."[11]

As we move from the industrial age to a digital age, we have entered a transition landscape that is anything but stable. Customer needs, wants, and behaviors are transforming each other at an unprecedented rate. We are seeing that organizations are not really as mechanistic as we thought, but are actually made up of people. We are seeing that the real purpose of businesses is to create value for people—a purpose that requires many people to accomplish. The value created by business takes the form of meaningful work for employees and desirable products or services for customers.

Public companies, however, downgrade the human being to a resource that can be sacrificed to short-term interests of shareholders and those who are supposed to exercise the stewardship of what Peter Drucker called the constitutive elements of modern society—our organizations and institutions skew this process of value creation by focusing sharply on efficiency. And they have increased this efficiency by using more and more computer algorithms—formulas for work that can be done more rapidly, efficiently, and predictably by a computer than by a human being. This strategy effectively places a bull's-eye on the back of every worker, allowing the next engineer to design a more efficient machine to take that job. This strategy defines a task-centered view of the organization, and allows the firm to scale up its functions almost indefinitely.

Unfortunately, these scalable institutions have a downside: Their consistency and predictability limit the organization's ability to try new techniques or ideas. The visionaries are pushed aside by the efficiency experts. To function in ways that promote creativity and satisfaction for workers, we need to move away from old industrial terms. These include Enlightenment notions of rationality, which are applied to both markets and workers. Industrial standardization has brought a division of roles, creating the dichotomies of consumer/producer, labor/management, and the

---

11 Ibid.

commoditization of workers to fill slots—in other words, universal fungibility.

Another negative feature of the old job market is that organizations restrict information about the status of employees. For example, mid-level managers abbreviate the information they have about employees before sending it up the chain of command. They may do this to minimize conflicting information or to reduce the options from which managers can choose, but the upshot is that opportunities for productive employer/employee conversation are reduced. Second, promotions are often based on an employee's ability to work within the existing system rather than to transcend that system and innovate. This reduces an employee's incentive to add value through creativity, even when there is a desire and path to do so. Third, the information available to mid-level managers is restricted; that is, just as the mid-level managers cannot pass on all information, they themselves do not have full information that could provide a basis for creativity.

A common belief among economists is that a continuous flow of new ideas, technologies, startups, and associated small businesses will generate a continuous demand for more workers. This is an appealing belief, but it rests on the outdated assumption that companies will continue to use the same old model of scalable efficiency. This is what machines are good at, and if it is our only strategy, we are right to worry about losing more jobs to machines. What we are lacking is not jobs, but imagination.

The New Job Market

A more constructive job market might rest on the premise that there are no useless people. To reach this viewpoint, we must agree that a healthy economy is one that lets people create value. If we as a society become as innovative in creating good jobs as we are in creating innovative products and services, we can sustain a more stable, fair, and collaborative economy.

Can the economy develop valuable jobs for every person, letting them do something that fits them like a well-tailored suit, pulling forth their talents, creating value and satisfaction for everyone involved? If so, there will be a very large number of job possibilities for a limited number of people. Eventually, people, not jobs, will be the scarce resource!

This will require a new view of work and a new job culture. Instead of getting a job because a company has a slot for which you seem qualified (and which a machine may someday learn to do better), you will get a job because people need other people around them, and they always will find ways of creating value for each other. How they might do this—by drawing pictures, cooking food, organizing closets, or organizing events—will be limited only by the imagination.

In mature, developed economies, demography is trending toward depopulation.[12] If this continues, the number of empty job slots requiring skilled people will continue to drop. This will increase the cost of labor in the traditional job market, which in turn will lead to more automation. This is different from the type of scarcity created by innovation tailoring jobs for people.

What kinds of policy would move us toward a new view of work? It can be policy that supports or mandates access to more and better information for job seekers. Currently, companies treat much of the information relevant to a job search (for example, compensation, benefits, working conditions, reporting structure, and real growth potential) as a strategic chip only to be revealed late in the bargaining process. This makes it practically impossible for candidates to compare more than a handful of job options, or to discover the best option until they have given their decision.

According to Tess Posner, the managing director of Samaschool, as many as 200 million people around the world lack access to

---

12 Philip Auerswald and Joon Yun, *Depopulation: An Investor's Guide to Value in the Twenty-First Century* (Kindle Edition, January 28, 2015), http://www. amazon.com/Depopulation-Investors-Guide-Twenty-First-Century-ebook/dp/ B00SW9JAHU.

the basic skills required to participate in the global digital economy and to earn a satisfactory wage.[13] Posner also notes that, although work through online platforms is growing by 22 percent each year, compared with 3 percent growth in offline jobs, many people are unaware of this opportunity and lack the basic skills to take advantage of it.[14]

A new job market opportunity is to prepare low-income people to succeed in the digital economy by providing online and instructor-led training in digital skills. It has been shown that a ten-week boot camp in online work can serve low-income populations across the world.[15] Such speedy transfer of skills is important in the new adaptive workplace.

In future successful work organizations, workers will be empowered and autonomous, teams will be interdependent and self-directed, and departments will communicate seamlessly. As Katz Kiely observes, "they will be incentivized to share knowledge and find solutions to complex challenges collaboratively."[16]

Definitions of Innovation

There are many different definitions of "innovation." Merriam-Webster defines it as "the act or process of introducing new ideas, devices, or methods" or, more generally, "the introduction of something new."

These definitions are not specific or inclusive enough to be useful in many important settings. Some definitions that fit different settings are:

---

13 Tess Posner, "The future of work is now: Why Samaschool is taking its curriculum online," *Samaschool News*, August 24, 2015, http://samaschool.org/the-future-of-work-is-now/.
14 Ibid.
15 Ibid.
16 Katz Kiely, "Companies are not machines," *LinkedIn Pulse*, June 26, 2015, https://www.linkedin.com/pulse/companies-machines-katz-kiely.

- A market economy: "Innovation is the creation and delivery of new customer value in the marketplace with a sustainable business model."[17]

- A society: "Innovation is the creation and delivery of surprising new knowledge that has sustainable value for society."[18]

- A culture: "Innovation is the introduction of a new narrative."[19]

These definitions are consistent in a variety of ways. First, new and sustainable customer value always introduces new knowledge into society. Second, every innovation introduces a new way of relating, and therefore a new narrative about a market economy, a society, or a culture.

A Common Language for Disrupting Unemployment

To discuss how to innovate for jobs and how to incorporate the synergistic roles of business, education, public policy, or any aspect of culture, we need a common language.[20]

There are no common narratives that can help people envision an innovation for jobs economy. Changing the narrative in any culture involves great faith in the methods of change and radical shifts in attitude and behavior.

Every innovation requires a name, so that we can refer to it; a definition, so that we know what it is or is not; and a narrative so that we can relate to it. In the 1980s, technology was seen as a barrier to innovation. In the 1990s, innovation was discussed in the

---

17 Curt Carlson, "Definition of Innovation," *Practice of Innovation*, March 2015 http://www.practiceofinnovation.com/definition-of-innovation/.

18 Curt Carlson, "Creativity and Innovation," *Practice of Innovation*, April 18, 2015, http://www.practiceofinnovation.com/creativity-and-innovation/.

19 Curt Carlson, "Innovation and Narrative," *Practice of Innovation*, April 10, 2015, http://www.practiceofinnovation.com/who-is-an-innovator/.

20 See John Hagel's chapter in this book, "Mobilizing Ecosystems to Drive Innovation for Jobs." Also see David Nordfors, "Innovation Means New Shared Language," in "Innovation Journalism, Attention Work and the Innovation Economy: A Review of the Innovation Journalism Initiative 2003-2009," *Innovation Journalism* 6, no. 1 (May 1, 2009): 18–21, http://www.innovationjournalism.org/archive/injo-6-1.pdf.

context of building products and business organizations. Today, innovation is virtually taken for granted in business, society, and the culture. A smartphone app can be built in weeks; a global organization with supply chain, sales, and delivery components can be set up by a one-person company in a day.

The barriers to innovation today are not those of technology but those of communication. There are companies with great products and business ideas that do not succeed, because they cannot communicate the value of what they are doing to customers. There are companies with many creative professionals who cannot create a good innovation, because they lack a common narrative.

The narrative is an essential part of an innovation, and shaping it is a part of the innovation process. Innovation journalism, communication, public discussion, social platforms, language, and research tools are all part of the innovation ecosystem. We cannot innovate faster than we can create new common language. The language has to be simple enough to bridge stakeholder groups, relevant and versatile enough to ideate innovations, and accurate enough to characterize and to form a blueprint for the innovations.

The innovation for jobs ecosystem needs a common language for a very eclectic variety of stakeholders, many of whom have not shared much language until now. Macro- and micro-economists, labor and innovation public policymakers, nonprofit and for-profit entrepreneurial organizations, philanthropists, and investors are among the many stakeholder groups that need to work together in the new ecosystem. A central task for these groups is to create a common language and a common narrative wherein everyone has an incentive to work with the others in disrupting unemployment and creating a successful middle class innovation economy.

Often, the best way to communicate innovation is through stories. According to neuroscience, informational text stimulates only two very small areas of the brain that process language and decode words into meaning. Information does not engage the range of functions that are used to tell stories: memories of texture, sensation, taste, emotion, physical movement, smell, color, shape, sound. Stories help share knowledge, drive action, and sustain communities. The ability and yearning to tell stories are at the core of what it means to be human.

Mismatches in the Labor Market

We are already hearing from many quarters about actionable ideas, policies, and approaches that amount to innovation for jobs. Examples include entrepreneurial initiatives to help people improve their earnings and do more meaningful work. These initiatives often use the entrepreneurial strategy of targeted training or retraining that allows employers to place or to promote people into jobs they are well qualified to fill.

The use of such strategies is still too rare, however, to counter the problem of unemployment, which is a grave challenge for the coming years. What are some reasons for this?

One set of problems flows from the gaps between labor supply and demand. For example, many jobs go unfilled—even though there are people who have the ability to do the work—simply because of insufficient or unavailable information. That is, the employer cannot reach the right employee, or vice versa.

Another issue is the mismatch between the jobs that are available and the skills that are required to perform them. Some skills are in very high demand, but the supply of workers with those skills is limited.

Another barrier is negative attitudes on the part of some employers. Even though many workers have the needed skills, they are not hired because of the powerful and often unconscious biases of potential employers regarding gender, ethnicity, physical features, educational background, or place of origin.

Solving these dysfunctions is part of our objective. It involves nothing more—or nothing less—than a shift from a world of push to a world of pull; a shift from firms' defining the jobs and deciding when to offer them to people's determining what they want to do and making it happen. Such shifts can have complex and powerful consequences that we cannot yet predict.

These shifts must take place in an evolving landscape of work. The pace of automation is accelerating, driven by rapid improvements in the price and performance of digital technology. Robots are displacing manual labor, while artificial intelligence and deep learning technologies are displacing humans from traditional white-collar, knowledge-worker jobs.

For the jobs that remain, the skills required to perform them are evolving rapidly. By some estimates, the half-life of a skill today has shrunk to about five years. If workers are to define their jobs, they continually have to upgrade their skills.

When looking to address the challenges ahead, we will find it helpful to review what we understand innovation to be. We already know about product and service innovation, as well as process and business model innovation. There are many more types, such as institutional innovation or new ways of interacting, and narrative innovation or new ways of relating.

As the development of digital infrastructures and the global liberalization of economic policy have increased the pace of change over the last forty years, the old infrastructures have struggled to adapt. Institutional innovation is trying to redefine the mission of institutions in the direction of innovation, flexibility, and inclusiveness. These changes are designed to celebrate new ideas, partnerships, and experiments. They are working toward a new, scalable learning that creates resiliency and can thrive in the face of rapid change. It means building creation spaces that help facilitate, rather than limit, interactions and relationships among workers, allowing organizations to increase the flow of information beyond cubicles and to increase learning and adaptability.

Where do the new people come from who will welcome the new ways of working in an idea-filled space that has no boundaries? Some features of Silicon Valley come to mind, but can we imagine a more general model? To provide an illustration, we have imagined a scenario with a company that recruits workers for just this kind of service, called "Jobly."[21] Using the same kinds of smart technology exploited by Google, Facebook, and other firms, Jobly is able to scan or even to infer a person's skills, talents, passions, experiences, values, and social network. It also is able to scan the employment market for activities that such a person might enjoy doing. The person might say, "I want to paint pictures, but I don't know how to earn money doing that." There is a fair chance that, among the billions of people on the planet, some people (or even just one) will be willing to pay someone to do that.

Or perhaps you try painting for a few weeks, then you try something else, until you find something that feels meaningful—maybe something you can do with other people you work well with. Using Jobly to find the right job is a bit like using a dating service to find the right partner. Along the way, Jobly helps you find courses to help you hone your skills so that you increase your employability. Jobly may also offer you health benefits by spreading the risk among many users. If Jobly takes a commission on what you earn, it has the incentive to make you as valuable as possible. You are the valuable service it offers to customers who buy work to create value.

Jobly would be disrupting unemployment by tailoring jobs to people who do not fit the available slots, the so-called unemployable. Other unemployables are people who have suffered disabilities, severe social challenges, or illness. In fact, we often find such people to be highly gifted, compassionate, or charismatic, making us feel that something must be fundamentally wrong with the dynamic of the labor market. With the right tools, the talents of unemployables can not only be discovered but also suitably matched with someone who values them. They may have less-than-obvious skills that have been strengthened by adversity or visible only when a certain need arises. These skills will seldom appear in the

---

21 Vint Cerf and David Nordfors, "How to Disrupt Unemployment," *i4j Blog*, July 23, 2014, http://i4j.info/2014/07/disrupting-unemployment/.

limited and narrow formats by which employers are accustomed to framing their employment opportunities.

The Boy and the Dolphin

A few years ago, one of us stayed in a coastal village on the Red Sea and witnessed an extraordinary relationship. It began with a Bedouin boy who was deaf and dumb from birth and had other developmental disorders. In any industrial economy, he probably would have been kept at home or institutionalized for life. But he was a good swimmer, and his parents brought him to the beach every day.

One day, his parents noticed that he had befriended a dolphin in the shallow waters near the beach. The boy and the dolphin became good friends, and the dolphin came to play with him every day. Beachgoers began to notice, and the dolphin and the boy began to welcome them into their play. The boy's family realized that the beachgoers were hungry and thirsty, and they started a seaside cafe and restaurant on the beach. Visitors came to eat and drink after playing with the boy and the dolphin.

The boy's unique ability had generated a new kind of work—or work-play—that helped provide a living for his whole family. This boy's unique and differentiated value could not be perceived by the traditional labor market, but was very real nonetheless.

The lessons are important: People can create value for one another. Despite misperceptions and biases, there are no useless people. We need an economy with a structure that allows people to see this and helps them create value. The problem is not one of too few jobs or too few problems to solve. There is plenty of work to do in reducing climate change, eradicating disease, and reducing violence—or in helping a boy befriend a dolphin.

How to Disrupt Unemployment

With a new mindset that appreciates the value of people, we can imagine how innovation can reduce unemployment or even drive it out of business. The problem is not that we lack innovation; it is that we are trying to run the new economy in the old way. If we become as innovative at creating good jobs as we are at creating innovative products and services, the innovation economy become sustainable. Today, there is a product or service being developed for every possible need and desire.

How can we reverse this so that a job can be developed for every possible talent and passion? Here again we look to the promise of digital and social media tools that can let us know that some of our contacts might be good entry points. If one of us decides to launch a project with a partner, Jobly will help find potential partners who are likely to have similar talents, needs, or passions. Jobly will locate the administrative tools to fix visas, permits, or licenses. Payments to Jobly, which resemble the fees collected by agents, will allow the firm to invest in continued refinement of its job-, worker-, and opportunity-mining techniques.

How big is the potential market for job innovation startups? Roughly $35 billion is spent each year on unemployment insurance in the United States. In comparison, all seed investments in startup firms each year amount to about 2 percent of that. Today, it is difficult to use federal labor funding to support innovation because of worries that innovation might kill jobs rather than create them. If innovation for jobs venture capitalists can show that their investments create more and better jobs than they kill, they could help break the barriers between labor and innovation policy. New policies could also provide incentives for private investors to create an innovation for jobs venture capital industry. They could do this for less than half a percent of what is spent on unemployment insurance, for example, by matching private capital in seed funds with an option for the private investors to buy them out. That could be enough to catalyze an industry that disrupts unemployment altogether.

Unemployment is costly not only in tax dollars—that is the smallest part of it. Human capacity is probably the world's most underutilized resource and the world's largest potential market. In an average Western country, only about half of all people are in the workforce, and about a tenth of them are officially out of work. This means that already in place is an economic force with enough potential power to double the gross domestic product.

Design Your Own Career?

Why isn't this happening already? As we suggested above, part of the problem is our tendency to frame the descriptions of both markets and workers using residual artifacts of industrial standardization. A more appropriate framework could be biological, or more precisely, ecological: the lion and the zebra, and the fox and the hare are mutually dependent, and they mutually select for one another from a vast ecological web of relationships. The notion of the artisan worker invites a biological or ecological analogy; that is, the artisan thrives in being unique in what he or she produces, but also relational in belonging to a larger network of artisans, all of whom do work that reflects a unique character and niche. This is the opposite of the fungible industrial worker. The artisan gains much from the networked digital economy: reduced costs of coordination, information, market discovery, and collective action. A sharing and cooperative economy has the potential to generate greater value than zero-sum transactions.

Giving people control over their identities and credentials is critical to generating a new job environment. In the "gig and guild networked economy," for example, we have what could be called a reputation economy. People should be the end nodes of peer networks; they should have control of their identities, data, and reputations; and they should be encouraged to form networked, loosely coupled organizations, federations, or guilds to share risks and resources. The decentralized Internet supports this direction through containerization, blockchains, and autonomous contracts and authorities.

We already know many people who design their own careers; they are sometimes called freelancers, consultants, or self-employed workers. Part of what they seek is a career that is more meaningful and satisfying. However, there are already a few private firms where employees are treated to as much or more independence as are the self-employed.

Such companies support a more organic growth, letting employees wend their way upward not by a straight career ladder, but by a kind of lattice. This respects and accommodates the worker's search for a better work-life balance, young parents' need to share child care duties, and boomers' desire to ease toward retirement. Success at such firms is defined not by achieving rank or seniority but by getting what matters to you personally and contributing to the work of others. This might require the ability to motivate and to reward people who are very different from yourself, or the ability to achieve collaborative decision-making with team members working in distant locations.

Fundamental to innovation for jobs is the desire to create business opportunities by raising the value of people who have little or nothing. This might be done through a competitive market for serving people, helping them earn sufficiently in the way that is best for them. The opportunities for people to do valuable things for one another are growing quickly as we develop more powerful tools for finding and matching. It is not difficult to imagine a Match.com dedicated to employment. The goal is to satisfy the customer, who in this case is the worker/earner. If social consciousness is aligned with business, if wealth generation is aligned with wellbeing, it changes the narrative.

The companies that can play successful roles in this new narrative will widen their focus from business-only to the collective good. Signs of success will include employees who are empowered and autonomous, teams that are interdependent and self-directed, and departments that communicate seamlessly. Every part of the organization, rather than working individually on problems, has an incentive to share knowledge and work collaboratively. The most successful digital transformations are done *with* people, not *to* them.

In the old world of work, the leader was known as the best, the holder of expertise in the organization. The people-centered firm, unlike the leader-centered firm, values the work culture in its entirety, and celebrates the power of all who share in its activities and goals. The culture, not the leader, is the human "operating system."

The new world of work will be characterized by people learning at whatever level is appropriate for them. They will understand that, if we learn faster, we might stay ahead of the machines that are learning our jobs so successfully, but that this is not really a solution as much as a segue into a new narrative where passion will be more important than training. For the old workplace, passion was often used to describe a hobby, but seldom a real job. In a people-centered economy, passion is more likely to be a central concern for the worker—and, hopefully, for the employer as well.

Jobs are a human activity: people relating to each other in a satisfying way. People have a need to relate in ways that create value, and this is one reason they need jobs. Different cultures have different values, and therefore, their job cultures may look different. This is a challenge for societies, but an opportunity for entrepreneurs, who can find ways of mediating cross-cultural communication. This level of innovation can boost empathy and cultural intelligence, as people learn to optimize work relationships to accommodate individuals with different values and belief systems [22]

The Algorithmic Economy

As management and computer science merge, we are moving into an economy powered by algorithms. Corporations are about management, but we are now learning that corporations also are

---

22 Murray Newlands, "Why Culture Matters For Startups - Q&A With Culture Influencer Cosmin Gheorghe," *Forbes*, June 22, 2015, http://www.forbes.com/sites/mnewlands/2015/06/22/why-culture-matters-for-startups-qa-with-culture-influencer-cosmin-gheorghe/.

cybernetic—meaning that they adapt to change as they move toward chosen goals. As cybernetics is part of control theory, and management is the practice of control, the two are merging in algorithms for managing corporations.

Psychology is creating algorithms for personalization, and sociology is using social data to become a computational science that studies how people interact. Algorithms are creating a new kind of understanding of how people and things relate, and new kinds of open organizations that are not centrally planned but grow and develop organically. Different systems can connect to each other organically through application programming interfaces.

The algorithmic economy is bringing new ways of seeing firms and looking at work. One example is the on-demand economy, in which workers find themselves on-demand gigs using mobile apps on their smartphones that match supply and demand for work. Instead of being employed, these workers have many different on-demand assignments. Will such work satisfy people's need for a good job? That, too, needs to be addressed by algorithms that can help people design portfolios of paid work that match their needs for a stable income. Insurance, taxes, and savings are already being managed by algorithms.

Future workplaces are increasingly managed by apps and algorithms, but it is not yet clear where employers or employees benefit most. Who will benefit if education and training certificates are replaced by performance-based reviews? How will people want to balance freedom and security, and what will that lead to? We can only design, test, and adjust along the way.

We might distinguish between the traditional economy and the creative economy, and note the difficulty experienced by old firms that try to join the creative economy. Some will make it while others will not. Old management practices are deeply entrenched.

One change we can already see is the rise in volunteer activities. No one is paid for working on Wikipedia or Linux, for example. There are few economic studies of this trend, in which people are paid in new ways, such as by gaining a sense of satisfaction or self-worth.

We may see an expansion of collective intelligence that is being driven by several different components. These may include the number of human beings, the number of people connected to the Internet, the quality of education or capacity building, the capacity to route individual attention to the correct problems and resources, the capacity to coordinate individuals as collective intelligences, and the fraction of our collective intelligence that is focused on an aspect of these problems.

All of these elements characterize a sharing, collective economy, a paradigm that must be driven by a change in our thinking about technology, ownership, incentives, and results.

Whatever the features of this new economy, people will need to earn money to support themselves. The platforms for paid work we see emerging are mostly about mass scale labor alignment, but they will not serve everyone. For example, people who are arrested but released even just once may have their arrest records maintained indefinitely, effectively grouping them with criminals and excluding them from all jobs, despite their innocence. For ex-convicts, the situation will be even worse in an algorithmic economy, which has the potential to create two new social classes: those below the application programming interface and those above it.

The People-Centered Economy

Some among us predict and even perceive another significant trend: the organizations that employ people will change the way they assign value to workers. Rather than viewing employees as expense items to be squeezed and cut into certain shapes, they will see them as resources capable of creating and delivering value to the organization. And this would not be the case only for what we now call knowledge workers—it would apply to all members of the organization, which drives home the point that every worker is ultimately capable of learning more and improving the performance of the organization. The less people are valued, the higher the probability that they have an ignored, underutilized capacity. We speak about ordinary people and the common man, but is there really any person who fits such descriptions? It may be more accurate to say that every person is unique.

When this is understood, employment trends may shift toward hiring more people to create more value, rather than hiring fewer people to cut costs. And rather than focusing only on the people within their organizations, businesses may systematically reach out and cultivate broader networks of participants. Rather than viewing outsiders as contractors to be squeezed, they might begin to view them as catalysts who can bring new ideas and help all of us learn faster in community. This scalable learning strategy might be called a people-centered view of the organization, one in which the organization adapts to the needs of each individual and helps him or her learn faster rather than bending the individual into pre-determined slots. Instead of asking, which person can perform this task? the people-centered firm asks, what is the most valuable thing this person can do? Previously, we didn't have the computing power or data to answer this question; now perhaps we have.

The people-centered economy may generate other ways of improving the work experience. The old employment model already faces substantial challenges from students and younger workers who hold different values than do previous generations. They are more likely to pursue "passion careers" and desire a job that is flexible and pays enough for them to pursue other goals. They also want a job that is more fun, and indeed, many startups have rebuilt old ways of doing work to provide more engagement and collaboration. Many younger workers value these characteristics above higher salaries.

For example, a person may be interested in Indian cooking, Egyptian archeological blogging, and regression analysis of health data. In the past, that would mean living a corporate life in a cubicle until retirement, at which time the person could pursue those interests. Today, one can easily imagine a set of opportunities that bring all those passions together. Startups are facilitating a much greater variety of work options, allowing everyone to choose the right mix of passion, salary, engagement, flexibility, and performance. As much as modern economic theory promotes specialization, the reality is that few people want to be confined to a single topic and ignorant of the rest.

We have wanted to see such a world for some time, but only recently have we had the algorithms and tacit knowledge to build people-centered systems. Massive advancements in computing, artificial intelligence, and communication are deleting millions of jobs in the United States alone. It is time for society to confront this situation head-on rather than trying to eke out profits from an antiquated full-employment system.

There will be deep debates about what algorithms should be allowed to do, and how much business risk should be borne by workers instead of by a company. Those debates are needed. Looking even further into the future, we need to ensure that workers can build a stable work life out of multiple small jobs—with health insurance and fair tax laws. We don't need to understand how innovation for jobs works in order to create exciting changes. But we can suggest scenarios, discuss them, and continuously tweak them to ensure that they do no harm and bring out people's hidden talents and hunger for learning.

A Learning-Intensive Society

Innovation combines learning and creating. Learning and creating rapidly are imperatives in the innovation economy and, thus, are necessary skills for humans who wish to transcend a traditional task-centered career. The maxim "fail fast to succeed early" becomes "learn fast to succeed early."[23]

---

23 Curt Carlson, "Innovation is Learning," *Practice of Innovation*, February 19, 2015, http://www.practiceofinnovation.com/innovation-is-learning/.

Innovation for jobs offers an opportunity for thinking about what we want that the current economy does not provide. These things include:

1. More fulfilling work that allows people of all generations to have a sense of purpose all their lives;

2. Help from others in achieving more fulfilling lives—in education, social services, environmental issues, transportation, housing;

3. Skills that make us more emotionally intelligent and socially intelligent, so we can collaborate together with more joy;

4. An understanding of how whole communities can distinguish themselves, perhaps holding an Olympics for communities instead of for individuals;

5. An understanding of what is important to us as humans—how to measure it and how to become more skilled at taking care of what is important to us.

We might consider separating actual needs from the "satisfiers" that our current model has developed. A subsequent step could be to look for new kinds of satisfiers that can meet those needs in the emerging environment. In this view, human beings do not need work per se; they need satisfiers. These include subsistence, protection, affection, understanding, participation, leisure, creation, identity, and freedom—qualities to be found in a new world of working.

We have pushed a number of these needs into the old view of work, but more often, work is a poor satisfier of these needs. We can't just do away with work, but we must innovate entirely new satisfiers. The key is to move legacy systems, such as education, out of the way while maintaining enough infrastructure to enable collaboration and to avoid chaos.

Information technology is fueling a learning-intensive society. We have never had markets fueled by information technology before. These markets are far more dynamic, allowing buyers and sellers to coalesce quickly. As demand shifts, workers have less time to adapt. This gives an advantage to those with better education and more exposure to entrepreneurial thinking and opportunities—which is not the majority of workers.

Schools are only recently beginning to let students bring their smartphones, by now our most important universal tool, into the classroom. It is not happening without controversy, since it is lowering the test scores of the students.[24] [25] The problem is that schools do not yet know how to teach good use of smartphones. Schools might catch up by working together with companies, such as Qualcomm, and their foundations, which are actively engaging in developing the field. According to Irwin Jacobs and Qualcomm "With more than 6.3 billion mobile connections worldwide, there is an extraordinary opportunity to leverage what has become the largest information and communication platform in history and transform education for the twenty-first century. Always-on, always-connected mobile devices in the hands of students have the potential to dramatically improve educational outcomes by providing ubiquitous access to learning resources and the ability to collaborate with peers and advisors in and out of the classroom."[26]

In a learning-intensive society, organizations must train more people in online skills. Only when all workers are prepared for a learning-intensive society can that society become truly inclusive, and only then will all workers become members of innovation for jobs.

---

24 "Schools that ban mobile phones see better academic results," The Observer, May 16, 2015. http://www.theguardian.com/education/2015/may/16/schools-mobile-phones-academic-results.

25 Louis-Philippe Beland and Richard Murphy "Ill Communication: Technology, Distraction & Student Performance" CEP Discussion Paper No 1350, May 2015, Centre for Economic Performance London School of Economics and Political Science.

26 Qualcomm, "Modernizing Education and Preparing Tomorrow's Workforce through Mobile Technology" White Paper presented by Irwin Jacobs at the i4j Summit 2013, http://i4j.info/i4j/menlo-park-2013/white-papers/modernizing-education-and-preparing-tomorrows-workforce-through-mobile-technology/.

Appendix: A Discussion in Bullets[27]

Challenges are Opportunities

Man vs. Machine

- The Internet of Things, machine learning, and robotics will disrupt many services, such as health care. Smart sensors and actuators can replace the need for many visits to the clinic. These technologies will kill many jobs. The same technologies can be used as tools for people, creating new opportunities for meaningful paid work.

Old Silos vs. New Realities: Power is Vertical, Potential is Horizontal

- Institutions: The innovation economy is taking off. The educational and employment systems are lagging.

- Innovation practices: Mature organizations develop silos that get in the way of innovation. This is a market opportunity for designing practices of innovation that work also for large organizations. Without these, corporations will have difficulties surviving in the innovation economy. The practice of innovation has become a discipline of its own.[28]

- Management: Good_innovation requires engaged and empowered employees. In this way, the market is providing incentive for humane management. A new creative economy is emerging from this shift in culture.[29]

- Governance: Labor economics and innovation economics are different silos, making it very difficult to formulate innovation for jobs policies. Governments are reluctant to spend unemployment benefits on innovation. Finance ministries want

---

27 An earlier version of this section was published within the report "i4j DC Paris: How to Disrupt Unemployment," Vint Cerf and David Nordfors, 2014, http://i4j. info/2015/03/i4j-dc-paris-how-to-disrupt-unemployment/.

28 Curtis Carlson and William Wilmot, *Innovation: The Five Disciplines for Creating What Customers Want* (New York: Crown Business Publishers, August 8, 2006).

29 Stephen Denning, "The Internet Is Finally Forcing Management to Care About People," *Harvard Business Review*, May 5, 2015, https://hbr.org/2015/05/the-internet-is-finally-forcing-management-to-care-about-people.

to know when and how jobs will be created. There are no accepted macroeconomic models for innovation creating jobs.[30]

- Economics: There is no language for innovation for jobs among economists. Labor and innovation economists publish in different journals and attend different conferences. Innovation economists study the microeconomy while labor economists look at the macroeconomy.[31]

- Journalism: Journalists who cover labor markets rarely cover innovation, and journalists who cover innovation rarely cover economics. Vertical habits in politics and journalism reinforce each other.[32] [33]

- Education: Many needed skills are not yet taught in schools; many taught skills are no longer needed. Teachers are trained to be specialists. Horizontal, multidisciplinary project work does not fit the vertically planned classroom system.[34]

- Recruiting: Managers want to hire people who can work across disciplines and stakeholder groups; standard employment processes are designed to find people who fit the available job slot.

Middle Class

- Organisation for Economic Co-operation and Development (OECD) member countries are in a middle class squeeze. People are being pushed out of the middle class. Since the 1980s,

---

30 "Vint Cerf, David Nordfors, Stefano Scarpetta, and Andrew Wyckoff, "Governments Need Policies Combining Innovation and Jobs," *i4j Blog*, September 1, 2014, http://i4j.info/2014/09/governments-need-policies-combining-innovation-and-jobs/.

31 Ibid.

32 David Nordfors and Sven Otto Littorin, "The 'Innovation for Jobs' Chasm" Huffington Post April 4, 2011, http://www.huffingtonpost.com/david-nordfors/lainnovation-and-job-crea_b_843872.html

33 David Nordfors "The Concept of Innovation Journalism and a Programme for Developing It," Innovation Journalism Publication Series 1(1), May 3 2004, http://innovationjournalism.org/archive/INJO-1-1.pdf.

34 Esther Wojcicki "Designing K-12 Education for the Innovation Economy" i4j Summit 2013 White Paper, http://i4j.info/i4j/menlo-park-2013/white-papers/designing-k-12-education-for-the-innovation-economy/.

wage gaps have widened in most OECD countries, even during times of job growth.[35]

- Meanwhile, the middle class is growing quickly in Asia, Latin America, and Africa.

- A paradox: Information and communication technologies are driving economic growth and decreasing inequality at the global level among countries, while at the same time contributing to rising income inequality within countries.[36]

Demography

- The world population is growing rapidly, but nearly every second person lives in a country where the workforce, and sometimes the population, is shrinking: China, Brazil, Europe and Japan.[37]

- Overall, the world population is aging,[38] but it is aging at a faster rate in wealthier nations due to healthier and longer lives and declining birth rates.

- All mature economies have aging populations. Labor markets are growing too slowly to meet future challenges.

Human Resources

- Youth in OECD member countries are the most well educated generation ever, but they still face an unemployment rate two to four times that of adults, despite the growing number of people aging out of the workforce.

---

35 Organisation for Economic Co-operation and Development, "Divided We Stand: Why Inequality Keeps Rising," December 2011, http://www.oecd.org/social/soc/dividedwestandwhyinequalitykeepsrising.htm.

36 Robert Pepper and John Garrity. "ICTs, Income Inequality, and Ensuring Inclusive Growth," in the "Global Information Technology Report 2015," *World Economic Forum*, http://www3.weforum.org/docs/WEF_GITR_Chapter1.2_2015.pdf.

37 Joon Yun, "The Next Black Swan: Global Depopulation", *Forbes*, December 6, 2012, http://www.forbes.com/sites/joonyun/2012/12/06/the-next-black-swan-global-depopulation/.

38 United Nations, Department of Economic and Social Affairs, Population Division, "World Population Ageing: 1950–2050," 2001, Chapter VI "Conclusions," 33–34, http://www.un.org/esa/population/publications/worldageing19502050/pdf/92chaptervi.pdf.

- Long-term unemployment is on the rise. People who are unemployed for more than a year are considered nearly unemployable.

- A paradox: With modern tools like smartphones, all people of all ages can create value. But in order to ensure a good professional career, people are discouraged from starting to work before they have finished college.

- In the world's leading economies, people are considered most employable between their twenties and forties. However, they are likely to remain able and healthy into their seventies and to live into their nineties.

New Economics for the New Networked World

Innovation disrupts economic models as much as it disrupts jobs. Action might actually perpetuate problems rather than solve them, because governments and business leaders use economics models that no longer work.

Here are excerpts from "New Economics for the New Networked World,"[39] organized by i4j/IIIJ at the Internet Governance Forum in September 2014:

- Business informatics: Internet information is now a part of decision making. Big data and open data change enterprise decision-making models.

  - Integration challenges: enterprise taxonomy, portal intranet database integration, data fusion, and linking for knowledge base.

  - Linking open data provides the following benefits: open standards and vocabularies, search and semantic content extraction, lightweight data integration, and several research projects.

---

39 David Nordfors and Elliott Maxwell, "New Economics for the New Networked World," Internet Governance Forum 2014, Workshop 194, http://www.intgovforum.org/cms/wks2014/index.php/proposal/view_public/194.

- We still do not have clear models for profit-sharing, cloud-based projects, because the transactions have the transnational characteristics of the Internet.

- Open government data is reliable and enables the creation of new businesses that are developing quickly.

- Businesses may be quicker than governments to adopt new economics tools, which can affect the split between applied microeconomics and macroeconomics.

- Access to data about the networked economy—for example, app development for cellphones—is much worse than access to data about the traditional industrial economy.

  - This can be critical since we need to understand what happens when small organizations in the networked economy disrupt sectors in the traditional industrial economy. One example is WhatsApp, a company with 300 employees acquired by Facebook for $19 billion. It disrupted the entire telecom industry, which employs many people. We need metrics that convey the winner-take-all aspect of the networked economy—metrics that we have not used in manufacturing and other areas where there is some equality/inequality within the company, but still a decent baseline. In the networked economy, we do not know where the bottom is or if anyone is earning profits.

  - An interim indicator for the networked economy can be job creation, but something more substantial is needed in the long run. To illustrate some major impacts, we need to address whether the networked economy is providing for more productivity growth than is measured in current statistics.[40]

---

40 This case is described by Google's chief economist, Hal Varian, in the story by Timothy Aeppel, "Silicon Valley Doesn't Believe U.S. Productivity is Down," *Wall Street Journal*, July 16, 2015, http://www.wsj.com/articles/silicon-valley-doesnt-believe-u-s-productivity-is-down-1437100700. One response to the productivity debate is the effort by the U.S. Bureau of Economic Analysis and the U.S. Bureau of Labor Statistics to develop better ways to measure what economists call "integrated" multifactor productivity. See Mark Dumas, Thomas F. Howells III, Steve Rosenthal, and Jon D. Samuels, "Integrated BEA/BLS Industry-level Production Account: Now Covering

- A lot of measurable, traditional business is disintermediated by Internet businesses that we do not know how to measure.

  - It is difficult to estimate the full impact of the Internet economy on GDP growth. There is an Internet paradox: "You can see the computer age[41] everywhere but in the productivity statistics."[42] This seems to apply to the networked economy as much as it applied to computers in the 1980s. Macroeconomists need numbers that show the link between policies and outcomes. Such numbers can be constructed by research. In one example, the OECD collected data on which countries' websites were hosted, and were able to link that data to the ease of doing business in those countries.

- The digital trace from people's cell phone usage, e.g., calling patterns, offers a wealth of data and possibilities for constructing new metrics and models.

  - This source of information might replace surveys over time.

  - It also brings up issues of property rights: Who owns the data? Who can sell data that is co-generated by users and network operators? It is fundamentally changing the traditional factors of production—land, labor, and capital—and how we quantify those factors and their value.

  - Telecom regulation becomes important for the development of economics when the telecom providers sit on massive amounts of data of interest to economists.

- Economics is almost discrediting itself as we see different economists addressing the same problem but coming up with very different results.

1998-2013," Bureau of Economic Analysis Briefing, September 2015, https://bea.gov/industry/pdf/indprodacctupdate982013.pdf. Robert Cohen of the Economic Strategy Institute is analyzing how the digital economy is changing productivity and jobs using a microeconomic approach in a project, "The Economic Impact of the 'New IP' and the Internet of Things: A U.S. and Global Forecast 2015 to 2025," to be posted at www.econstrat.org.

41 For a discussion of the computer age, see "Information Age," *Wikipedia*, https://en.wikipedia.org/wiki/Information_Age.

42 Robert Solow, "We'd Better Watch Out," *New York Times Book Review*, July 12, 1987, page 36.

- The reason you can use so many different models in this digital economy is that so many things are not right in the classic economic models.

  - For example, many classic economic models assume the economy stays at equilibrium. Yet we have seen that, in many cases, disruptive technologies are cutting costs considerably each year.

  - Traditional economics assumes individuals are motivated primarily by making or saving money. But with social media, we are finding that those economics do not always explain people's behavior. People spend huge amounts of time because they receive psychic rewards, or are part of a team in a game, or like to be part of a community. New economic models need to take into account these broader psychological kinds of compensation.

- National statistics organizations need new roles in the new networked economy.

- Much data of emerging importance is controlled by private big data companies, such as Google or Facebook. It is of growing interest to governments to access and understand that data, but companies may not want to share it.

Re-defining Jobs as a Need

- Benefits that provide security for workers, such as pensions, health insurance, and so on, are connected to employment.

- A high cost of unemployment for the middle class is the loss of these benefits when there are no obvious alternatives.

- The average lifespan of an S&P 500 company has shrunk to about fifteen years. People must now switch jobs at the right time or have diverse sources of income—such as their own businesses or freelance work—to spread the risk.

- We might define a job as what people mean when they say, "I need a good job." Someone with a good job can pay the rent and raise kids without having to worry all the time. This is an important need, and it needs a name.

- But a job can be many things: full-time employment, self-employment, freelancing, or a mix of these. Whatever makes people feel engaged and appreciated, enables them to pay their bills, and makes it possible to raise kids without having to worry about poverty is a good job.

The Future of Matching People and Jobs

Imagine that Jobly has modules that help in various ways to match people and jobs. What can these modules be? And which methods can be constructive? Several of them already exist.[43]

Methods

- **Artificial intelligence** is helping us with extracting ideas and other features from unstructured data, searching, matching, adaptation, automation, and language processing.

- **Social network analytics** lets us understand people's skills and interests, and the ways they interact. They also identify the importance of various topics in a discourse and point out pathways toward a goal.

- **Big data analytics** can help make sense of the world and its multiple contexts, and map out ideas, trends, and markets.

- **Personal big data analytics** shows people the patterns in their own corpus of email, social media, browsing history, health, and well-being. This helps them understand which of their experiences, interests, passions, talents, and contacts are important in different contexts.

- **Predictive job matching** amplifies the resume and background with personality and cultural fit.[44]

---

43 Rick Wartzman, "The Wildly Ambitious Future of the Job Search," *Fortune*, March 19, 2015, http://fortune.com/2015/03/19/job-search-future/.
44 Ben Baldwin, "The Next Generation of Hiring is Job Matching," *Wall Street Journal*, November 26, 2014, http://blogs.wsj.com/accelerators/2014/11/26/ben-baldwin-the-next-generation-of-hiring-is-job-matching/.

- **Collective intelligence** achieves power through crowdsourcing (e.g., Wikipedia), crowdfunding (e.g., Indiegogo), and networking (e.g., Facebook, LinkedIn).

Modules for Strengthening People

- **StrengthsFinder** helps people discover their unique combination of strengths. Today this can be done by survey, as in the Clifton StrengthsFinder.[45]

- **Skills training and education** cultivate identified strengths, as the massive open online course Coursera does for people with education and Samaschool[46] does for people without education.

- **Passion finder** helps people discover what they really want to do. Career life can smother people's natural ability to seek rewarding and valuable activity. Scalable methods, such as the startup Passion Company, are being developed.

- **The self-efficacy developer** cultivates people's trust in their own abilities or in a basic competence that needs to be developed. Self-assessment, featuring trust, self-understanding, and low transaction costs, can replace testing, as in the SanderMan profile.[47]

- **Reward for empathy and values** helps people maintain empathy and good values in rewarding ways. Empathy and good values are increasingly important in a creative economy in which people are rewarded by compensation other than money.

- **Lifestyle planner** helps people plan their time and set their priorities for greater stability and predictability.

- **Narrative coaching** might become more important than the CV. Job requirements and skills come and go, but the character of individuals and the chemistry among people in teams

---

45 To learn more about the Clifton StrengthsFinder, see https://www.gallupstrengthscenter.com/.

46 To learn more about Samaschool (formerly SamaUSA), see http://samaschool.org/.

47 To learn more about SanderMan, see http://v37.sandermancloud.com.

are enduring and vital. A networking economy needs people who can create narratives about themselves and their interests. Storytelling may also increase insight, effectiveness, and engagement.

- **Mentor matching** offers a meeting place that pairs people with mentors. For example, Pave.com is developing a market for mentors.

- **Social meeting places** provide peer support.

- **Learning and maker programs** convert empty buildings into public venues with resources, including maker tools, computer labs, online classes, networks, and shops for people to create things (Tech Shops) which they sell the in the marketplace (Etsy).

Modules for Finding Opportunities

- **Career profiler** shows the present state of careers: required skills and commitments, in-demand skills, career paths, salaries, available jobs, demographics and satisfaction rates among professionals. The company discovery platform Craft. co has aggregated more than 50 million datapoints on 250,000 companies, including vacancies, team profiles, and key performance indicators.

- **Career concierge** recommends jobs, Amazon-style. If the user likes one job, Jobly discovers and suggests other jobs the user might like.

- **Volunteering** brings many things of value to people and society that cannot be priced or lack business models. People may be more inspired by work that lacks quantifiable output. Products and services provided by volunteers will sometimes become commercial alternatives, such as the Firefox browser, the Linux operating system, and Wikipedia.

Modules for Matching People and Opportunities

- **"Dating service"** entrepreneurs and companies often seek out people who have skills, talents, and personalities that align with a team and a mission rather than a career title.

- **Skills translator** helps translate experience from one context to another so job seekers and hiring managers can bridge differences in vocabulary. Hiring managers struggle with this issue and end up hiring the wrong people or overlooking great candidates. A translator could help organizations understand a person's skills in terms that are recognizable and relevant, and could help people see how these skills can be applied in a new context. For example, street smarts are often as important as book smarts; someone from the streets has the skills to think outside the box in order to survive, and those skills can be used in entrepreneurship. A college student who majored in psychology might be perfect for the marketing field, an aura healer might find herself a position in a human resources department, or a hardworking bartender with the ability to learn new skills may become a hardware engineer—and be more successful than an applicant with traditional credentials.

- **Virtual world matching** provides a safe environment for prospective employees to experience company culture, to make mistakes, and to assess their fit as team members. It also encourages new positive social behaviors.

- **Cross-cultural communication facilitator** helps overcome cultural barriers in team building, enabling teams to leverage on diversity.

- **Merits extractor** points to personal data that indicate skills, experiences, talents, and passions that can match a specific job and can be measured against a "social graph" that suggests contacts who might be helpful as references or advisors.

- **A shift in focus from employment to employability**[48] entails doing work that creates value, getting paid for it, learn-

---

48 For a discussion of employability, see "Employability," Wikipedia, https://en.wikipedia.org/wiki/Employability.

ing new skills, and enhancing the ability to find work in the future.

Other Services

- **Company starter** makes it easy for entrepreneurs to start businesses with little overhead cost. This is already happening with open source software, Google's free product suite (Docs, Spreadsheets), free conference call services, affordable website builders, Mechanical Turks, microtasking (Fiverr. com), and business mentoring (Clarity.fm, Score.org).

The Future of Economics and Policy

Economics and Analytics

- **New economics for the networked world** measures the economy in a way that counts how the networked economy is changing both existing and emerging firms. This should provide a new set of measures that might also support analysis in real time to identify new trends and clusters without making assumptions. It also creates approaches to estimate the contribution of the networked economy to prosperity and economic health through:

  - Connectedness

  - Data flows across international borders

  - Well-being and happiness

Finally, it creates metrics to articulate the value of volunteer and collaborative work (e.g., Wikipedia and Linux). One place this has been discussed is the Internet Governance Forum IGF 2014.[49]

- **Narrative analysis** is studying what people are talking about (a robust form of sentiment analysis, for example) as a complement to the number-centric analytics that dominates

---

49 David Nordfors and Elliott Maxwell, "New Economics for the New Networked World," Internet Governance Forum 2014, Workshop 194, http://www. intgovforum.org/cms/wks2014/index.php/proposal/view_public/194.

today. There are enormous volumes of discussion available for analysis, such as the websites of Google News, Twitter, and Facebook.

Some Policy Fields

- **Innovation for jobs** provides greater incentives and resources for job seekers, including those who have been laid off, to discover their own particular talents instead of competing with oversubscribed job openings. People who are laid off often survive on insurance benefits rather than using this time to develop existing skills or to discover new ones. A percentage of unemployment insurance budgets could be used to fund job startups, similar to the way the Small Business Innovation Research program funds startups, or to match private capital in venture funds investing in innovation for jobs. A model is the Israeli government's Yozma-program, which bootstrapped the Israeli venture capital industry by merging labor, technology, and education policies.

- **Baseline security** can reduce risk for freelancers and the self-employed. Workers need regulation, an intermediary, or self-insurance, including health services and education for themselves and their families. The Danish flexicurity concept proposes that people with guaranteed baseline security will be less fearful about switching jobs, making the labor force more flexible and more responsive to the requirements of the innovation economy.

- **Empathy and basic values** must be fundamental qualities of societies in constant flux. In a versatile innovation economy, very small groups of people can create enormous value or cause enormous damage. The more empowered people become, the more important empathy becomes. Values depend on culture, which can accelerate or retard the efforts of entrepreneurs.

- **Malicious practices** must be identified and addressed promptly and continuously. For example, Jobly could help former drug dealers translate experience into legitimate careers, but also could recruit people to criminal activity.

- **Public statistics/economics** will be essential for the future of good governance, which will require access to statistics and big data that are not controlled by national statistics organizations but by private companies. Government might need access to data to improve public services, but companies will be unwilling to share it. This will apply especially when governments aim to use the data in ways that can compete with, or otherwise affect, the business of the company owning the data.

- **Public perception** of job seekers needs to change. Instead of viewing job seekers as losers who have fallen out of the job force because of underperformance, we should reframe our view of job transitions as normal and even positive opportunities to discover new talents. A person who has had four jobs in quick succession might be more resilient and adaptable than someone who has stayed in an unrewarding position for ten years.

Some Open Standards and Services Provided by Third Parties

- **Portable reputation** lets employees carry their work record from one marketplace to another so they can maximize their earnings instead of starting from scratch every time they enter a new marketplace.

- **Skills certification** offers proof that a worker's skills are authentic by allowing registration of relevant facts, including education and employment history. Imagine a Carfax-like service for jobs—a Jobfax.

i4j Activities 2013-2015

- i4j web site: http://i4j.info_

i4j Summits 2015

- **i4j Mountain View, February 26–27, 2015**[50]

  - Organized by the i4j chairs, Vint Cerf, Google, and David Nordfors, IIIJ

  - Venue: Google headquarters

- **i4j DC Leadership Forum, September 1, 2015**[51]

  - Organized by Vint Cerf, Google, and David Nordfors, i4j

  - Venue: Google, DC

- **i4j UK Parliament, November 19, 2015**[52]

  - Organized by Lord Jim Knight, House of Lords, and David Nordfors, i4j

  - Venue: House of Lords, Parliament of the United Kingdom, London

i4j Summits 2014

- **i4j Yearly Summit, Menlo Park, Silicon Valley, March 17-18, 2014**[53]

  - Organized by Vint Cerf, Google, David Nordfors, IIIJ, and Sven Littorin, IIIJ

  - i4j Executive Partners: FIRS, Google, SITRA, SRI International

  - i4j Challenges: How can we accredit marketable skills? How can we design and finance public services? How can

50 See http://i4j2015.i4jsummit.org/.
51 See http://i4j.info/2015/07/i4j-dc-project-plan/.
52 See http://i4j.info/i4j-uk-parliament-participants/.
53 See http://i4j.info/i4j/i4j-menlo-park-2014/.

the Internet of Things increase personal health and job creation? How can innovation disrupt unemployment?

- **i4j Skåne, Sweden, June 2–3, 2014**[54]

  - Organized by Pia Kinhult, First Governor of Skåne (Southern Sweden), Per Eriksson, President of Lund University, and Sven Littorin and David Nordfors, IIIJ

- **i4j Paris, September 6, 2014**[55]

  - Executive workshop, maximum twenty-five participants

  - Organized by Stefano Scarpetta, Director of the OECD's Directorate for Employment, Labour and Social Affairs; Andrew Wyckoff, Director of OECD's Directorate for Science, Technology and Industry (STI); and David Nordfors and Vint Cerf, IIIJ

  - Venue: U.S. Embassy, Hotel De Talleyrand, hosted by Daniel Yohannes, U.S. Ambassador to the OECD

- **i4j Washington, D.C., October 13–14, 2014**[56]

  - Organized by Vint Cerf, Google, and David Nordfors, IIIJ

  - Venue: National Academy of Sciences, Washington, D.C.

- **i4j Helsinki, Finland, December 4–5, 2014**[57]

  - Organized by Mikko Kosonen, CEO, SITRA, the Finnish Innovation Fund, and David Nordfors, IIIJ

- i4j Summits 2013

- **i4j Inaugural Summit, Menlo Park, Silicon Valley, March 2013**[58]

  - Organized by Vint Cerf, Google, and David Nordfors, Sven Littorin, and Anders Flodström, IIIJ

---

54 See https://www.delegia.com/app/attendee/default.
   asp?ProjectId=&PageId=31247.
55 See https://www.youtube.com/watch?v=xcSDYYrkr5A&feature=youtu.be.
56 See http://i4jdc.i4jsummit.org/.
57 See http://i4jhelsinki.splashthat.com/.
58 See http://i4j.info/i4j/menlo-park-2013/.

- **i4j Munich, Germany, November 2013**[59]
  - ▲ Organized by Aart De Geus, President and CEO, Bertelsmann Stiftung, Bertram Brossardt, General Manager vbw-Bayern, and David Nordfors, IIIJ

- **I4j Team and Advisors**

i4j CO-FOUNDERS AND CO-CHAIRS

Vint Cerf
Vice President and Chief Internet Evangelist Google, co-inventor TCP/IP

David Nordfors
CEO, IIIJ Foundation

ADVISORS

Anders Flodström, co-founder i4j, President Emeritus KTH Royal Institute of Technology

Sven Otto Littorin, co-founder i4j, CEO, Serio, former Swedish Minister for Employment

Monique Morrow, CTO – Evangelist for New Frontiers Development, Cisco

Stefano Scarpetta, Director, Employment, Labor and Social Affairs, OECD

Dane Stangler, Vice President of Research and Policy, Ewing Marion Kauffman Foundation

Jacob Ziv, President Emeritus, Israel Academy for Science and Humanities

Esther Wojcicki, founder of Palo Alto High School Media Arts Program and vice chair of Creative Commons.

---

59 See http://munich.i4jsummit.org/#&panel1-

2013-2015—ADVISORS EMERITI

David Arkless, Founder and CEO, Arklight Consulting; Aart De Geus, Chairman and CEO, Bertelsmann Foundation; **Tim Brown**, CEO and President, IDEO; **Curtis Carlson**, President, SRI International; **Herman Gyr**, Founding Partner, EDG Enterprise Development Group; **Per-Kristian (Kris) Halvorsen**, Chief Innovation Officer, Intuit; **Irwin Jacobs**, Founding Chairman and CEO Emeritus, Qualcomm; **Pia Kinhult**, First Governor of Skåne, Sweden; **Mikko Kosonen**, CEO, SITRA Finnish Innovation Fund **Robert Litan**, Director of Research, Bloomberg Government; **Joaquim Oliveira Martins**, Head of Division, Regional Policy Development, OECD; **Heather Munroe-Blum**, President Emerita, McGill University, Professor of Medicine, **John Voeller**, Senior Vice President, Black & Veatch.

(Titles and affiliations at the time they served)

PRESENT FOUNDING AND EXECUTIVE SPONSORS

Cisco

Ewing Marion Kauffman Foundation

Google

OECD

CHAPTER 1

The Bifurcation is Near[1]

By Philip Auerswald[2]

Abstract

The fact that digital computers are able to outperform humans in accomplishing mental tasks should come as no surprise: they were designed to do just that. However, this fact alone does not suggest that human work of all types is on a trajectory toward automation and ultimately displacement. The actual impact of digital disruption on the future of work will depend critically on the nature of the work itself—which is to say, the *how* of production, and not just the *what*. Tasks that are routine and can be easily encoded will be performed by computer; those that are not will continue to be performed by people. The answer to the question, "Is there anything that humans can do better than digital computers?" will turn out to be fairly simple: humans are better at being human.

Introduction

Two decades ago, futurist Jeremy Rifkin published a book titled *The End of Work: The Decline of the Global Labor Force and the Dawn of the Post-Market Era,* in which he argued that we should be deeply

---

1   This chapter is derived from *The Code Economy,* forthcoming from Oxford University Press in 2016.
2   Philip Auerswald is an associate professor at the School of Policy, Government, and International Affairs, George Mason University.

concerned about the social impact of digital technologies. "We are entering into a new period in history—one in which machines increasingly replace human beings in the process of making and moving goods and providing services," he cautioned.[3] "A near-workerless world is fast approaching."[4]

In the past four years, a number of prominent economists and technologists have taken up Rifkin's argument in one form or another. They include Erik Bryjolfsson and Andrew McAfee, Tyler Cowen, and Martin Ford. From an economic standpoint, their argument is straightforward:

1. The power of technology is growing at an exponential rate.

2. Technology nearly perfectly substitutes for human capabilities.

3. Therefore, the (relative) power of human capabilities is shrinking at an exponential rate.

If they are correct, we should be deeply worried, indeed, about the process of digital disruption.

In sharp contrast, Ray Kurzweil's 2005 best-seller, *The Singularity is Near: When Humans Transcend Biology*, argued that the exponentially increasing power of technology—particularly, though not exclusively, digital computing technologies—will trigger an epochal discontinuity in the human experience. From an economic standpoint, Kurzweil's argument is comparably straightforward:

1. The power of technology is growing at an exponential rate.

2. Technology nearly perfectly complements human capabilities.

3. Therefore, the (absolute) power of human capabilities is growing at an exponential rate.

Like many others, Kurzweil argues that "only technology can provide the scale to overcome the challenges with which human society has struggled for generations."[5] But he goes further,

---

3   Jeremy Rifkin, *The End of Work* (Los Angeles, CA: Tarcher, 1996), 12.
4   Ibid., 106.
5   Ray Kurzweil, *The Singularity Is Near: When Humans Transcend Biology* (New York: Viking, 2005), 371.

tracing the arc of technologically-enabled progress forward into the immediate future to sketch the outlines of "The Singularity," which "will result from the merger of the vast knowledge embedded in our brains with the vastly greater capacity, speed, and knowledge-sharing ability of our technology, [enabling] our human-machine civilization to transcend the human brain's limitations of a mere hundred trillion extremely slow connections."[6] When it comes to algorithmically-empowered robots taking our jobs, Kurzweil's prescription is straightforward: If you can't beat 'em, join 'em—maybe even literally, in cyborg fashion.

So which is it to be for humanity: Rifkin's dystopian World without Work or Kurzweil's bright Singularity?

The Origin of Digital Disruption

The fact that digital computers are able to outperform humans in accomplishing mental tasks should come as no surprise: they were designed to do just that. When the United States was thrust into World War II in December 1941, all types of inputs into the war effort were suddenly in short supply: rubber, oil, iron ore, and, of course, human computers.

Human computers were just people doing math. They were needed to perform computational work of a military variety—particularly the generation of firing tables, used by artillerymen to set aim on enemy targets. At the Ballistic Research Laboratory—the U.S. Army's primary weapons testing facility in Aberdeen, Maryland—the demand for this specialized labor was so great that the military established a secret unit called the Philadelphia Computing Section (PCS) at the University of Pennsylvania's Moore School of Electrical Engineering. The army recruited one hundred human computers, mostly women, from the University of Pennsylvania and neighboring schools.[7]

---

6   Ibid., 20.
7   George Dyson, *Turing's Cathedral: The Origins of the Digital Universe*, (New York: Vintage, 2012), 69.

The PCS turned out to be far from adequate to the task.[8] By August 1944, Herman Goldstine, a mathematician and army lieutenant who acted as the liaison between the Ballistic Research Laboratory and the PCS, lamented, "The number of tables for which work has not yet started because of lack of computational facilities far exceeds the number in progress. Requests for the preparation of new tables are being currently received at the rate of six per day." Goldstine had not, however, placed all his bets on the PCS. A year earlier, he had been prompted by a colleague to seek out John Mauchly, a physics instructor at the Moore School, who had written a memorandum proposing that the calculations being performed by PCS workers could be completed thousands of times more rapidly employing a digital computer built with vacuum tubes. Goldstine obtained funding for Mauchly's proposal and, shortly thereafter, he engaged the great mathematician John von Neumann to lead its implementation.[9] The effort to construct the world's first general purpose digital computer was underway. On February 14, 1946, less than six months after the end of World War II, the Army announced the completion of the Electronic Numerical Integrator and Computer (ENIAC).

---

8   As George Dyson reports in his comprehensive account of the development of the digital computer, "A human computer working with a desk calculator took about twelve hours to calculate a single [ballistic] trajectory.... To complete a single firing table still required about a month of uninterrupted work." *Turing's Cathedral*, 69–70.

9   Goldstine did not know that von Neumann was part of another secret military team, working in the desert of New Mexico on the design for the atomic bomb.

Figure 1 caption: Programmers Betty Jean Jennings (left) and Fran Bilas (right) operate ENIAC's main control panel at the Moore School of Electrical Engineering.

ADDITIONAL INFORMATION: Betty has her left hand moving some dials on a panel while Frances is turning a dial on the master programmer. There is a portable function table C resting on a cart with wheels on the right side of the image. Text on piece of paper affixed to verso side reads "Picture 27 Miss Betty Jennings and Miss Frances Bilas (right) setting up a part of the ENIAC. Miss Bilas is arranging the program settings on the Master Programmer. Note the portable function table on her right.

The ENIAC set into motion a transformation in work and life on a global scale that continues to accelerate today. But that first general purpose digital computer also very directly eliminated about a hundred jobs—those of the Philadelphia Computing Section. Those initial victims of digital disruption were caught up in larger events—world wars and the like—that obscured the historic nature of their particular circumstances. Yet, as digital computers have become ever more powerful, they will inevitably outperform humans in an expanding range of tasks, challenging the viability of an ever-growing list of occupations of which "human computer" was but the first.

Among the economists and analysts who have written about this process, the one who most clearly understood its implications was also—perhaps unsurprisingly—the one most directly involved in bringing about digital disruption to begin with: Herbert Simon.

From Ideas to Algorithms

Herbert Simon was a person of rare ability and achievement. The only person ever to receive both the A.M. Turing Award from the Association for Computing Machinery and the Sveriges Riksbank Prize in Economic Sciences in Memory of Alfred Nobel, Simon was at once a foundational contributor to behavioral economics and a pioneer in the field of artificial intelligence, his achievements having included the construction of the first computer program to defeat a human at chess.[10]

As a graduate student at the University of Chicago studying municipal administration, Simon had taught himself to use a punch card computing machine to generate statistical tables. Later, during World War II, he met John von Neumann and got an inkling of the top secret work under way on the ENIAC. Just a decade later, Simon was at the frontier of the development of the computer as a general purpose problem-solving machine.

In January 1956, Simon walked into a beginning-of-the-semester session for one of his courses at Carnegie Mellon University and announced, "Over the Christmas holiday, Al and I invented a thinking machine."[11] It was true: Simon and his colleague Al

---

10 Herbert Simon and Allen Newell, "Heuristic Problem Solving: The Next Advance in Operations Research" reprinted from *Operations Research* 6, no.1 (January-February 1958), https://www.u-picardie.fr/~furst/docs/Newell_Simon_Heuristic_Problem_Solving_1958.pdf

11 Hebert Simon, *Models of My Life,* New York: Basic Books, 1991. p. 206. In making his classroom pronouncement, Simon was slightly ahead of himself in that the LT wasn't actually running on a computer at the time he made his claim. However, as Simon later recalled, "we knew precisely how to write the program." That is where Simon's family came into the picture. Shortly after the classroom episode, Simon gathered his wife and three children together at his office because he needed their help "running" the LT program. Simon described their involvement as follows:

> While awaiting completion of the computer implementation of LT, Al and I wrote out the rules for the components of the program (subroutines) in English on index cards, and also made up cards for the contents of memories (the axioms of logic). To each member of [my family] we gave one of the cards, so that each person became, in effect, a component of the LT computer program—a subroutine that performed some special function, or a component of its memory. It was the task of each participant to execute his or her subroutine, or to provide the contents of his or her

Newell had been the first to realize the vision that the mathematician Gottfried Leibniz had expressed almost three centuries earlier for "a general method in which all the truths of reason would be reduced to a kind of calculation."[12] The program was called the Logic Theorist or LT. It was the first program ever developed to simulate human intelligence.

Comparative Advantage

Slightly more than a decade after the construction of the first digital computer and more than half a century ahead of the most recent writing on digital disruption, Herbert Simon fully grasped the potential for computers to replicate the capabilities of human problem-solvers. In a paper written in 1960, he makes the following startling claim: "The fact that chess programs, theorem-proving programs, music-composing programs, and a factory-scheduling program now exist indicates that the conceptual mountains have been crossed that barred us from understanding how the human mind grapples with everyday affairs. It is my conviction that no new major ideas will have to be discovered to enable us to extend these early results to the whole of human thinking, problem-solving, and decision-making activity."[13]

Furthermore, well ahead of his peers, Simon understood that "automation" would extend well beyond the factory floor: "We should not make the simple assumption that the higher status

---

memory, whenever called by the routine at the next level above that was then in control.

So we were able to simulate the LT with a computer constructed of human components. Here was nature imitating art imitating nature.

In this manner, Simon's wife (not a trained mathematician) and his three children, then ages nine, eleven, and thirteen, were able to prove the first twenty-five or so theorems in Alfred North Whitehead and Bertrand Russell's *Principia Mathematica*. That evening of family fun in 1956 launched the field of artificial intelligence.

12 From *De Arte Combinatoria*, a work Leibniz published in 1666, based on his doctoral dissertation. Leibniz was the co-inventor of calculus, among other achievements.

13 Herbert Simon, "The Corporation: Will It Be Managed by Machines?" in. M. L. Anshen and G. L. Bach, eds., *Management and the Corporations 1985* (New York, NY: McGraw-Hill, 1960), 48.

occupations, and those requiring the most education, are going to be the least automated. There are perhaps as good prospects technically and economically for automating completely the job of a physician, a corporate vice-president, or a college teacher, as for automating the job of a man who operates a piece of earth-moving equipment."[14]

Yet Simon also understood intuitively what research since has demonstrated:[15] as the power of computers increases, work bifurcates. What this means is that, following the economic principle of comparative advantage, computers perform those tasks most readily subject to algorithmic definition while humans perform those tasks most resistant to algorithmic definition.

In short, Simon foresees a process by which the processes of work bifurcate, with humans focusing on those tasks in which their (our) skills are *comparatively* strong, and computers focusing on those tasks in which their skills are comparatively strong: "We conclude that human employment will become smaller relative to the total labor force in those kinds of occupations and activities in which automatic devices have the greatest advantage over humans; human employment will become relatively greater in those occupations and activities in which automatic devices have the least comparative advantage."[16] At every stage in this process, technology not only partially substitutes for human capabilities but also generates new kinds of human requirements and capabilities.[17]

---

14 Ibid, 35.
15 See e.g. David Autor, Frank Levy, and Richard Murnane, "The Skill Content of Recent Technological Change: An Empirical Exploration," *The Quarterly Journal of Economics* 118, no. 4 (2003), 1279-1333. More on this below.
16 Simon (1960), p. 24.
17 I thank Jordan Greenhall for emphasizing the importance of this dimension in personal communication. The dynamic Simon describes here naturally leads to a situation in which any technological unemployment that occurs is transient, and the economy is generally at full employment, but importantly where "full employment does not necessarily mean a forty-hour week, for the allocation of productive capacity between additional goods and services and additional leisure may continue to change as it has in the past. Full employment means that the opportunity to work will be available to virtually all adults in the society." (Simon 1960, p. 23) Furthermore "automation does not mean 'dehumanizing' work. On the contrary, in most actual instances of recent automation, jobs were made, on the whole, more pleasant and

The core point I seek to make in this chapter is that such disruptions follow a predictable pattern: The creation of a new high-volume, low-price option creates a new market for a low-volume, high-price option. Every time this happens, the introduction of a new technology forces a bifurcation of markets and of work.

From Idea to Algorithm

Innovations begin as an idea and end as an algorithm. In each stage, the work associated with the innovation bifurcates, in the manner described by Simon.[18] In his paper for this volume, Geoff Moore generalizes from such stories. At each stage from invention through repeated innovations to automation and digitization, new value is created and the role of the human worker is redefined. As figure 3 illustrates, early in the introduction of a new good or service, work is conducted by entrepreneurs organized in a guild-like model, each of whom has at least some ability to perform every task in the production process. As processes become and tasks better defined, specialization occurs and it is possible to break up tasks into a value chain. As tasks are further specified and stages of work are algorithmically defined, work can be performed in an assembly line model. In the limiting case, every element of a production process can be algorithmically specified, and entire process is automated.

---

interesting, as judged by the employees themselves, than they had been before." (Simon 1960, p. 27)

18 In the case of the LT simulation I described in footnote 9 above, the progress was rapid: Simon and Newell had an idea for a process to prove theorems. The idea started in their heads. They then transferred the idea to notecards. The notecards specified standardized operating procedures—subroutines in a larger production algorithm—that allowed the work to be distributed, and thus performed more quickly.

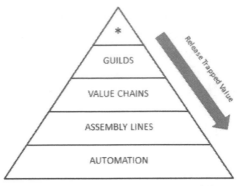

Figure 2 caption. Geoffrey Moore's model of the progressive redefinition of work through progressive stages of automation. Source: Moore (2016), in this volume.

As Moore notes: "At the end of any arc of innovation, when we have gone all the way from entrepreneur to automation, goods and services that used to be scarce and very expensive to acquire have now been made plentiful and cheap. That makes them a perfect platform upon which to build the next wave of innovation. Entrepreneurs are the ones who catch on to the implications of this new state the fastest. They kick off the next round of innovation, they launch the next arc." The journey from idea to algorithm thus arguably typifies the evolution of any technological innovation and the new work it creates.

Consider the evolution of the personal timekeeping industry. In the seventeenth century, when the watch industry was new and production was centered in London, Paris, and Lyon, watch buyers regarded the first Swiss watches much as Americans viewed Japanese cars in the 1970s—as products that were crude compared to those manufactured at the established production enters, but also redemptively cheap and functional. Consequently, also like Japanese cars, the early Swiss watches found a market niche and sold well.

In Geneva, following the pattern prevalent in other industries, the successful watchmakers soon organized themselves into a guild. Their aim was to govern market entry and restrict competition among existing firms. As the city prospered further from the watch trade, incumbent producers successfully enacted laws that excluded both immigrants and women from employment in watchmaking and reserved work in the trade exclusively for *citoyens* (citizens) and *bourgeois* (burghers). An interval of remarkable, if concentrated, prosperity for Geneva ensued.

Figure 3 caption. Earliest known dated watch (1530).

ADDITIONAL INFORMATION: The watch is engraved on the bottom: "PHIL[IP]. MELA[NCHTHON]. GOTT. ALEIN. DIE. EHR[E]. 1530" (Philip Melanchthon, to God alone the glory, 1530). There is no watchmaker's mark, although Nuremberg is considered the birthplace of spherical watches (called "Nuremberg Eggs"). A single winding kept it running for 12 to 16 hours, and it told time to within the nearest half hour. The perforations in the case permitted one to see the time without opening the watch. This watch was commissioned by the German reformer and humanist Philip Melanchthon (1497–1560).

Footnote source: https://en.wikipedia.org/wiki/Watch#/media/File:German_-_Spheri cal_Table_Watch_(Melanchthon%27s_Watch)_-_Walters_5817_-_View_C.jpg]

As the industry continued to develop, however, the city faced a challenge: with watchmaking talent among the citoyens and bourgeois already fully employed, how could the watchmaking industry continue to grow without relaxing the restrictions on employment that had helped watchmakers earn their high incomes and elevated social standing? The solution, of course, was to outsource. (If you're starting to read "Geneva circa 1650" as "USA circa 1995," you're getting the subtext.) Rather than permitting immigrants or women to be employed in the workshops of

Geneva, the Swiss sent watchmaking work out to people living in the poor villages and towns in the Jura Mountains—inconsequential places, including one by the name of Neuchâtel. The guilds held little sway in these mountain villages. Therefore, paying no mind to Genevan employment restrictions, producers in Neuchâtel and elsewhere in the Jura organized production around a model that suited their circumstances and predispositions. Rather than bringing workers together in a single workshop, they broke the work down into repetitive tasks, gaining production efficiencies that could best be attained by a division of labor. Once the door of opportunity was opened to the shepherds of the Jura, they did not hesitate to rush through it.

Fast forwarding to 1967, it was in Neuchâtel, at the Centre Electronique Horloger (CEH), that the first prototype quartz wristwatch was unveiled. In Japan Seiko unveiled a quartz wristwatch the same year. Quartz watches were as accurate as mechanical timepieces but far easier to construct. By the 1980s, quartz wristwatches had come to dominate the market. They were produced by the millions on assembly lines. Reliable time became a commodity. As early as 1982, the journal Assembly Automation published a paper titled "Robots start to assemble watches."[19] By the 1990s, mobile phones began to be sold widely, and for many people replaced watches. Timekeeping became one app among many on a smartphone—software, not hardware.

The process from idea to algorithm was complete. It had spanned 500 years.

Did this end the Swiss watchmaking industry? Not exactly. True, Switzerland—once the dominant watchmaking nation—today produces fewer than 5 percent of the timepieces manufactured for export globally: Switzerland exported 29 million in 2014, as compared to China (the global leader in terms of volume), which exported 669 million. But what of value? There the story is different:

---

19 John Hartley, "Robots start to assemble watches", *Assembly Automation* 3, Iss: 3 (1983),169 – 170.

Swiss watch exports were worth $24.3 billion in 2014, nearly five times as much as all Chinese watches combined.

The industry had bifurcated.

One Technologically-Induced Bifurcation after Another

As you may have guessed, I am going to propose that, in addition to the limiting-case arguments offered by Rifkin and Kurzweil, a third line of argument is possible:

1. The power of technology is growing at an exponential rate.
2. Technology only partially substitutes for human capabilities.
3. Therefore the (relative) power of human capabilities is shrinking at an exponential rate for those categories of work that can be performed by computers, and not for others.

The best evidence to support this line of argument comes from the labor market studies conducted by Harvard economist Richard Murnane and MIT economists David Autor, Daron Acemoglu, and Frank Levy, and presented in dozens of papers and one book co-written in various combinations and with co-authors over the past dozen years. In a seminal 2003 paper published in the *Quarterly Journal of Economics*, Autor, Levy, and Murnane summarize their findings as follows:

We argue that computer capital (1) substitutes for a limited and well-defined set of human activities, those involving routine (repetitive) cognitive and manual tasks; and (2) complements activities involving non-routine problem solving and interactive tasks. Provided these tasks are imperfect substitutes, our model implies measurable changes in the task content of employment, which we explore using representative data on job task requirements over 1960–1998. Computerization is associated with declining relative industry demand for routine manual and cognitive tasks and increased relative demand for non-routine cognitive tasks.[20]

---

20 "The Skill Content of Recent Technological Change: An Empirical Exploration," p. 1279.

From the Autor, Acemoglu, Levy, and Murnane perspective, the impact of digital disruption on the future of work depends critically on the nature of the work itself—in other words, the *how* of production, and not just the *what*. Tasks that are routine and can be easily encoded will be performed by computers, where those that are not will continue to be performed by people. The jobs of the human computers at the Philadelphia Computing Section are a case in point: Because the human computers were literally performing rule-based logical computations that are the essence of computer "programs," they were also literally the first people to lose their jobs to digital computers. That process is ongoing.

Where Kurzweil talks about an impending technologically-induced Singularity, the reality looks much more like one technologically-induced bifurcation after another. Furthermore, the answer to the question, is there anything that humans can do better than digital computers? turns out to be fairly simple.

Humans are better at being human.

What Can Humans Do Better Than Computers?

If there is one place in the United States that defines the implosion of the manufacturing-based economy in the United States, it is Detroit, Michigan. Detroit's challenges are so well known that they do not require recounting. But one Detroit story that is worth telling has to do with a recent manufacturing success story—one that doesn't have to do with cars, but with a consumer technology that is much older: watches.

In a building that once housed the General Motors design studio, craftspeople at a four-year-old company called Shinola hand-assemble high-end watches from Swiss parts. The company has grown rapidly in the two years since its founding; in its third year it assembled 150,000 high-end watches and earned $60 million in revenue. Its success is due in equal measure to the quality of its hand-assembled product and the power of its story. It gives its employees and its customers an opportunity to be part of an undertaking that conveys a purpose beyond the actual requirements of minute-to-minute time tracking.

If Shinola's success seems like an anecdotal aberration, unreflective of larger trends, then consider again what happened to the Swiss watch industry after the introduction of the low-cost, high-reliability quartz watch. Were it not for market bifurcation, the Swiss watch industry would have disappeared, crushed by the low-cost and high-volume capacity of Asian producers. Yet, to the contrary, as we saw above, quartz watches did not lead to the elimination of the mechanical watch industry. Instead, the creation of a new high-volume, low-price option created a new market for a low-volume, high-price option. The introduction of a new technology forced a bifurcation of markets and of work. This process is the norm, not the exception, whenever technology disrupts work.

We can take this as far back as we like. Technologies of agriculture forced bifurcation of work. Technologies of trade forced bifurcation of work. Technologies of manufacturing forced bifurcation of work. Technologies of industrial organization forced bifurcation of work. Now, technologies of automation and artificial intelligence are doing the same.

Because work is fundamentally algorithmic, it is capable of almost limitless diversification through both combinatorial and incremental change. The algorithms of work become, fairly literally, the DNA of the economy. Such bifurcations can, and do, occur without limit.

The question, therefore, is not whether opportunities for meaningful work will exist but how they will be compensated. As Geoff Moore puts it, "Digital innovation is reengineering our manufacturing-based product-centric economy to improve quality, reduce cost, expand markets, increase profits, and reward investment—all of which are very good things. It is doing so, however, largely at the expense of traditional middle class jobs. This class of work that is bifurcating into elite professions that are highly compensated but outside the skillset of the target population and commoditizing workloads for which the wages fall well below the target level."[21]

In the next round of digital disruption, the high-volume, low-price option may yield such minuscule margins that the profits will derive almost entirely to platform owners. Even if not, however, there is good reason to expect that the low-volume, high-price option will contain most of the distributed opportunities for profit in the economy.

In order for this process to continue into the future—that is, in order for the Bifurcation to outpace digital disruption—three conditions must hold:

- Combining these conditions allows for work to bifurcate endlessly and for new processes (which is to say, new work) persistently to earn a profit consistent with a living wage. Through this vehicle, the greatest opportunities for new work enabled by digital disruption may be those most seeming distant from digital technology itself. These include, but are not limited to:

- The farm-to-table movement (including slow food and all re-localization extensions)

- The maker movement (including handmade crafts)

- The wellness movement (including health care to the home, mindfulness, and biohacking)

Whether this is precisely the right list or not is beside the point. The central message is that the greatest opportunities created by digital disruption may have nothing directly to do with digital technology.

Entering Unmapped Territory

In one fundamental respect, our era is different than any before: Because the world is becoming more prosperous, population

---

21 Moore (2016), in this volume.

growth has slowed and in many places is reversing. Over 40 percent of the world's population already lives in nations with sub-replacement fertility, defined as a fertility rate below 2.1 children per woman.[22] This list includes all of North America, all of Europe, all of East Asia (notably including China), and additional populous countries including Brazil and Iran. What this means is that, absent immigration and the demographic impact of increasing lifespans, populations are already declining in all of these regions.

There is no historical analogue to the coming era of global population decline. Why not? Because in our era, population decline has been caused not by war, disease, and famine, but rather by increased prosperity. In all of human history, this has never before happened. No books, plays, or poems exist to guide us in an era of prosperity-driven population decline. It is new.

John Stuart Mill predicted two centuries ago that human society ultimately would reach a stage in which a stagnant population earns high (relative) incomes and has steadily improving well-being, all sustained by continued investment in research and development. John Maynard Keynes offered a similar vision in a 1930 essay titled "Economic Possibilities for our Grandchildren," in which he predicted that humanity was on a trajectory to solve the problem of economic scarcity within a matter of decades. Keynes maintained that humanity's problem thereafter would be to solve the problem of leisure time, noting that "it is fearful for the ordinary person, with no special talents, to occupy himself, if he no longer has roots in the soil or in custom or in the beloved conventions of a traditional society." In such a world, the promise of meaningful occupation ultimately comes to be valued above wealth for its own sake, and returns from income are correspondingly subject to diminishing returns.

---

22 The total population of Europe, including Russia and non-EU countries, peaked in the year 2000. Japan is well into population decline, and many more countries are on the brink. And recent data from the National Center for Health Statistics show that the U.S. birthrate fell for the sixth straight year in 2013, to an all-time low.

Because of the uniqueness of the coming era of depopulation, it is not easy to analyze its implications. Nonetheless, as Joon Yun and I argue in our recent eBook, *Depopulation: An Investor's Guide to Value in the Twenty-First Century*,[23] there is good reason to believe that the trajectory of human progress will continue over the century to come, even as global population begins to decline.

A combination of population decline and population aging suggests a powerful coincidence of needs: as the human population plateaus in the aggregate, continued improvements will require individuals to exhibit greater levels of creativity across the population, and across a human life, than has ever been the case in the past. Some of that creativity will contribute to aggregate growth through improved productivity and new innovations, while an even greater share will contribute to solving what Keynes referred to as the problem of leisure— what we might today think of as the challenge of living a meaningful, fulfilling life.

But what if the Singularity arrives in full force, and "computers" evolve into sensing, thinking, feeling, loving beings completely indistinguishable from humans—into full-fledged immigrants from the future?

Herbert Simon has something to say about that as well: "I am confident that man will, as he has in the past, find a new way of describing his place in the universe—a way that will satisfy his needs for dignity and for purpose."[24]

He has a point.

---

23 Philip Auerswald and Joon Yun, *Depopulation: An Investor's Guide to Value in the Twenty-First Century* (Kindle Edition, January 28, 2015), http://www.amazon.com/Depopulation-Investors-Guide-Twenty-First-Century-ebook/dp/B00SW9JAHU.

24 Herbert Simon, *The Shape of Automation for Men and Management*, New York: Harper and Row, 1965; p. 52.

CHAPTER 2

The First Software Age: Programmable Enterprises Creating New Types of Jobs

Robert B. Cohen, PhD[1]

Abstract

Programmable enterprises are developing their businesses around cloud computing, big data, and the Internet of Things. They will employ millions of people in new types of jobs. Examples of such jobs are continuous service delivery jobs where employees become skilled generalists and part of DevOps teams, data analytics teams, and jobs related to sensor ecosystems. A very conservative estimate is that spending on these new infrastructure jobs could create about five million new employees between 2018 and 2023, and perhaps fifteen to twenty-five million jobs by 2033. These jobs represent not only talented and very skilled workers, but also substantial numbers of managerial, support, and marketing employees.

The Programmable Enterprise: The Motor Promoting Dramatic Job Change

---

1   Robert Cohen is senior fellow, Economic Strategy Institute and Director, Project on the Economics and Business Impacts of the New IP and Internet of Things. http://econstrat.org/research/the-new-ip-and-the-internet-of-things.

Programmable enterprises are distinguished by new, open, extensible, and interoperable computer and communications architecture they have deployed and continue to expand. Some of the best examples are Amazon, Google, Facebook, Apple, Baidu, Alibaba, Box, and Twitter. In addition, a number of traditional enterprises are making considerable efforts to become programmable, including UPS, Boeing, GM, BMW, Wells Fargo, Bank of America, and Intel.

These businesses expect to flourish because they can create new services and applications for customers and suppliers. Programmable enterprises are characterized by the innovative architecture they depend upon, virtualization and cloud computing and the changes that have made them more capable of supporting new service functions and processes. These services were once extremely difficult to deploy. With today's innovative infrastructure and software, firms can use these new ecosystems to deploy sophisticated data analytics as well as software platforms to design and enhance innovative services and the value of services they plan to deploy in the future.

Three trends shape the evolution of these firms:

1. The adoption of cloud computing and a shift of applications to a software-defined cloud environment.

2. The development sophisticated, real-time analytics that link operational tools and processes to applications.[2] In part, this is driven by the tremendous growth in mobile applications.

---

2   Chris Anderson, "The End of Theory Will the Data Deluge Make the Scientific Method Obsolete?" *Edge - The Third Culture*, June 30, 2008, http://edge.org/3rd_culture/anderson08/anderson08_index.html. Anderson argues that scientific methods based upon "grand theories" are not likely to survive the emergence of big data. He says the petabyte world "calls for an entirely different approach, one that requires us to lose the tether of data as something that can be visualized in its totality. It forces us to view data mathematically first and establish a context for it later." I would argue that we are likely to find new and innovative methods to analyze and visualize big data. I am not sure I would agree with Anderson's conclusion. I think new mathematical and visualization techniques will enable us to visualize data in its entirety.

3. Moving into sensor ecosystems and the Internet of Things. This dominates retailing, firms with a web presence, such as Amazon, eBay and Twitter, but also is significant for Facebook, Apple and others. It is key for firms that maintain and control equipment or services, such as Ford and GM for driverless cars and Boeing for sensor-controlled aircraft services. This trend will affect health care, but not until many operational and data privacy issues are resolved.

The programmable enterprise is highly people-centered because its central purpose is connecting people and responding to their needs. As the MetLife case that follows shows, big data analysis will be at the heart of the programmable enterprises' economy.

MetLife[3] has moved rapidly to establish itself as a provider of services, going beyond merely selling insurance. It has focused much of its transformation on its ability to gather large amounts of data on policyholders and their environment. So MetLife possesses not only data on the policyholders themselves but also information about the places they live, the health care in their communities, the local climate, and other factors.

With big data analysis tools, MetLife created a "wall" for all of its policyholders. The information available on the wall requires sophisticated data management tools and links. Using the wall, a MetLife employee can respond to a policyholder's call and see in a single window all of the policyholder's recent interactions with MetLife. This allows timely and comprehensive service without the usual delays.

But MetLife has not only created a better way to respond to customer inquiries, but also employed new technologies to develop new ways to use data analytics. This includes tools such as Apache Hadoop and MongoDB[4] that help it gain greater insight into its big data lakes.

---

3 This case draws upon information in Derrick Harris, "The Promise of Better Data has MetLife Investing $300M in New Tech," GigaOm Research, May 7, 2013, https://gigaom.com/2013/05/07/with-300m-earmarked-for-tech-innovation-metlife-wants-to-remake-insurance/.

4 Derrick Harris, "The Promise of Better Data has MetLife Investing $300M in

In addition, because of its command over big data, MetLife can do what other firms, such as Netflix, already do.[5] It can see what answers groups of users habitually request when they call for policy information. It can offer them different bundles of services or policies and see what helps them and what does not. It can evaluate what is going amiss when policyholders or customers terminate their policies, and then try to correct the flaws customers perceive. It can also analyze the behavior of specific populations of policyholders or groups within the population.

So, the analysis of big data and the creation of new services is central to the programmable enterprise. These firms differ from others because they have:

1. A unique architecture for their enterprise computing and networking, based broadly upon open systems and standards—software defined infrastructure—with easy "end-to-end" connectivity.[6] This architecture facilitates resource sharing and the rapid creation of new services.

2. The ability to analyze and to manage enormous amounts of data.

3. The ability to create new services based upon the innovative architecture and data analytics they use.

4. The development of a number of software and services platforms, within the organization and outside of it, to distribute and manage existing, emerging, and future services.

Building on these innovative capabilities, the programmable enterprise represents not only talented and very skilled people, but

New Tech," GigaOm Research, May 7, 2013, https://gigaom.com/2013/05/07/with-300m-earmarked-for-tech-innovation-metlife-wants-to-remake-insurance/.

5   Discussion with Adrian Cockcroft of Battery Ventures, formerly at Netflix, at the Open Network Users Group (ONUG), Columbia University, May 2015. Netflix has created a wealth of new services for customers to enhance their viewing of streaming video and respond to customers' tastes.

6   ONUG is a group that is championing this approach. Many of its members, including major banks and financial firms, insurance companies, retailers, and logistics firms, have led the move to deploy these systems.

also substantial numbers of managerial, support, and marketing employees. These employees[7] will probably account for thirty to sixty percent of a programmable enterprise. The engineering and research, operations, information technology, and information systems staff will account for about forty to seventy percent of employees, with the higher percentage more likely for startups.

In addition, through secondary impacts, these firms probably create jobs in related services or industries that have substantial multiplier impacts of their own. Professor Enrico Moretti[8] has estimated that Silicon Valley firms create a disproportionate number of legal and engineering jobs, as well as a large number of personal service jobs.

Thus, the jobs created by new programmable enterprises are likely to include more than just IT jobs. In their secondary or multiplier impacts, these firms are also more likely to create a wide range of jobs outside of information technology.

The new architecture for business does several things that will affect jobs and the pattern of employment:

1. It creates new jobs, such as DevOps or platform teams that combine software creation and design, software testing, software deployment, storage and networking skills. This is an example of a hybrid job, but it also indicates that the new jobs in the emerging economy will be far more skilled than they have been in the past. Rather than providing tasks, new jobs will demand a range of skills.

---

7   Jigsaw.com profiles accessed June 2, 2015, and Codingvc.com, "Analyzing Angel List Job Postings, Part 1: Basic Stats," September 8, 2014, http://codingvc.com/analyzing-angellist-job-postings-part-1-basic-stats. See Robert Cohen, "A Software-Defined Economy: Innovation, the Internet and Future Growth: Describing Enterprise-based Innovations Driving Change," Columbia Institute for Tele-Information's conference, "The Impact of the Internet on Employment: Creating Winners and Dealing with Losers," Columbia University, June 5, 2015.
8   Enrico Moretti, *the New Geography of Jobs* (Boston: Houghton Mifflin Harcourt, 2012), and Leslie Brokaw, "The Multiplier Effect of Innovation Jobs," *MIT Sloan Management Review*, June 6, 2012. http://sloanreview.mit.edu/article/the-multiplier-effect-of-innovation-jobs/.

2. It employs services to create new value in the economy. These companies run innovative new services on the new computing and networking architecture. They exploit new software platforms to expand the innovative, new functions they offer.

3. Software and services become the defining features of these firms. As a consequence, they improve their productivity by using software to control and manage software based systems. Programmable firms also introduce machine learning and robotics in production and couple this with data analytics. The dominant change is the primacy of software and services in such enterprises.

A number of new types of jobs will emerge from these trends:

1. Programming jobs and support for "continuous service delivery" and the creation of microservices. These positions usually merge old technology competencies, so a "platform engineer" may need to know about DevOps (software programming), networks, and storage. In some cases, jobs that formerly required only business knowledge—for example, a job as a data center manager—will probably need to require more technical skills and "hands-on" experience with new data analysis tools such as Hadoop.

2. Data analytics teams that must perform rapid analyses and set up data visualization and reports on trends and new directions. This requires higher-level competency with new database tools, such as Hadoop. It also requires additional lower-level jobs to assemble and manage the data and translate the analysis into understandable discussions or reports.

3. Jobs related to the use of sensor ecosystems. These jobs will expand due to the building and deployment of ecosystem infrastructure, particularly computing, storage, and networking at the edge of large enterprise or public networks. These ecosystems will most likely evolve through several stages, so the building will not end in the first phase of building but

will require several stages of rebuilding to add more capabilities. Jobs from sensor ecosystems also will expand due to the addition of data analysts and managers to support the retailing, web, and maintenance firms that will be big early users. Major areas of expansion will be data analytics (extending big data analytics, mentioned above), computer security, and software development.

Estimating the Jobs Created by Programmable Enterprises

The estimate of jobs presented here is based upon two changes in the economy. First, that there is an increase in the number of cyber-physical systems—groups of coordinating computational elements controlling physical entities—in both the manufacturing and services side of the economy. Second, the growing importance of the services side of business—essentially the "Googlization" of the economy—as firms make services an ever more important part of their sales. So auto firms not only gain better control of manufacturing process and supplier networks from cyber-physical systems, but sell cars based on the package of services they offer buyers, as Tesla does. They also benefit from sensor based services that can tell drivers the location of the nearest charging station when their battery needs to be recharged. The same holds for aircraft manufacturers such as Boeing where services to airlines matter as much as or more than the quality of the aircraft they sell; resolving systems issues in real-time using connected networks is as much a part of selling planes as producing aircraft.

We can create a very rough estimate of the jobs and economic impact of programmable enterprises by assuming that a major increase in spending on software defined infrastructure occurs over the next five years. If there are about 160 million jobs in the U.S. economy and the gross domestic product (GDP) is roughly $18 trillion, there are roughly ten million jobs for every trillion dollars of GDP. We estimate GDP as the sum of consumer spending, investment and growth, so every dollar of new investment increases GDP. As a consequence, in order for large banks to implement new cloud computing and virtualized infrastructure, we estimate that they need to spend more to build a new infrastructure to re-place the old; this requires about $2 billion per year for five years. The sum means banks make $10 billion investments each for thirty or forty banks, or about $300 to $400 billion of new investment. This would add about $400 billion to the economy and create about four million new jobs. Another estimate would be that if half of the Fortune 500 spend about $1 billion per year over five years to become programmable enterprises and implement new software-defined infrastructure, they would make investments of $1.25 trillion and would create about 12.5 million new jobs.

If we take a conservative estimate for 2018 to 2023, this would mean about 5 million jobs over 5 years. If there are follow-on initiatives to expand the deployment of this new infrastructure because of the high value it produces for enterprise users, it is possible that there might be additional rounds of investment on a similar scale. This could result in successive waves of new jobs in succeeding years. It would mean that 5 to 10 million jobs might be created during each successive five-year period, or perhaps fifteen to twenty-five million jobs might be created over a fifteen-year period. There also would probably be some loss of jobs as the new infrastructure replaces an older one, but the conservative estimate might encompass such a job tradeoffs.

Are there similar forecasts that suggest such a dramatic change in employment and GDP? Yes, Boston Consulting Group (BCG) has forecast similar impacts in its study of Industry 4.0.[9] BCG's analysis is based upon the efficiencies that data analytics and connected sensor networks will provide for German manufacturing. It finds that over 10 years, Internet 4.0 will drive productivity gains of 5 percent to 8 percent on manufacturing costs as well as raise German GDP by 1 percent per year over 10 years.[10] The increase in GDP will create as many as 390,000 jobs and add as much as 250 billion euros to manufacturing investment.

---

9 Michael Russmann and others, "Industry 4.0: The Future of Productivity and Growth in Manufacturing Industries," April 2015. www.zvw.de/media.media.72e472fb-1698-4a15-8858-344351c8902f.original.pdf

10 Russman and others, page 2.

If we adjust the BCG estimates to take into account the fact that they only cover the manufacturing economy in Germany, or, only 30 percent of the total economy, and assume that similar changes are likely to occur in the service sector, then Germany would add 833 billion euros (or $908 billion) in total investment and as many as 1.3 million jobs.

If we adjust these estimates so they are roughly scaled to impacts for a US economy that is five times as large as Germany's, the U.S. economy might add as much as $4.5 trillion to US GDP and 6.5 million jobs using the BCG forecast.

There are some reasons why the BCG study's estimates are smaller than the rough estimate I presented above. First, BCG estimates that there will be a twenty-year transition to Industry 4.0. I assume a more rapid transition for the US economy. BCG's analysis appears to be influenced by changes in the auto industry and its suppliers, but its economic impact analysis does not seem to encompass the move to services linked to connected cars and driverless cars. My picture of more substantial spending by the Fortune 500 assumes a much wider and transformative change in US infrastructure over the next 10 years than BCG does.

Conclusion

This paper argues that changes in infrastructure based on the virtualization of computing and networking will transform businesses. Programmable enterprises will exist in a world that revolves around software and services. This will dramatically change the types of jobs people perform. These changes will occur very rapidly, and traditional training mechanisms will be unable to adjust. This will open new categories of jobs for people who lack formal degrees. Employers such as Microsoft[11] are already moving people to the types of jobs that will be needed in this new economy and providing them with new skills to function effectively.

---

11 James Staten, "It's Not the Technology, It's you," OpenStack Silicon Valley 2015 Conference, Mountain View, CA, August 26, 2015, https://www. openstacksv.com/2015-archive/2015-videos/.

A very conservative estimate is that spending on these new jobs would create about 5 million new employees in the sectors mentioned between 2018 and 2023, and perhaps 15 to 25 million jobs by 2033. Productivity gains and price reductions related to these new industries would create additional economic benefits that are more difficult to estimate but might be very sizable. This is particularly true of benefits generated by the demand elasticity effects related to reductions in prices for a wide range of services, including telecommunications.

CHAPTER 3
Mobilizing Ecosystems to Drive Innovation for Jobs

By John Hagel[1]

Addressing the jobs challenge is one of our greatest opportunities for achieving sustained prosperity for us as individuals and as a society. The challenge is formidable, because it has so many different dimensions and is rapidly evolving on so many different fronts. Addressing this kind of challenge is well beyond the capability of any single individual or even any single institution, no matter how powerful, smart, and, endowed with resources they may be. Successful approaches to the jobs challenge will require the creation and evolution of more encompassing ecosystems that are intentionally organized to mobilize and to focus many diverse participants. But the challenge is so great that it is well beyond the capacity of even a single ecosystem—it will require many different ecosystems to emerge and collaborate in increasingly complex ways.

To accomplish all of this, we will need to craft a compelling narrative that can motivate a growing number of participants with diverse capabilities to come together in relevant ecosystems and to address elements of the challenge while keeping in focus the much broader opportunities created by tackling this challenge. As we'll see, narratives are different from stories in that they are

---

1 John Hagel is a consultant and author who specializes in the intersection of business strategy and information technology and Co-Chairman, Center for the Edge, Deloitte & Touche.

a compelling call to action, making clear that the attainment of a very attractive opportunity hinges on our choices and actions.

Framing the Jobs Challenge

So, what is the jobs challenge? Often, our discussions about the jobs challenge quickly narrow to focus on one small part of the much larger challenge. Rather than looking at the entire elephant, we get consumed by the part of it that is nearest to us and thereby lose sight of the bigger, and growing, challenge, ahead of us.

This is completely understandable, because so many elements are contributing to the larger challenge that we face. First, the global workforce is continuously growing—the number of people who are willing and able to work is increasing. We have parts of the world with an aging population and a growing number of older people who, either out of necessity or out of a desire to remain productive, do not want to retire from the economy.

And we also have large numbers of people who have either dropped out of the workforce or continue to seek work without success, either because they lack the necessary skills, because they are victims of various forms of bias (e.g., women and members of various ethnic or religious groups), or because there are simply not enough openings to accommodate all of the applicants. The paradox is that, at the same time, many institutions are complaining that they can't find enough qualified people to fill the positions available, reflecting the mismatch between available skill sets and evolving skill needs.

As if all of that weren't challenging enough, we have the dynamics that are intensifying the jobs challenge over time. Robots and artificial intelligence technologies are claiming more jobs that used to be performed by humans. And the rapid evolution of our businesses and economies is rendering old skills obsolete and generating demand for an entirely new set of skills that are in very short supply.

Our educational systems are falling behind in their ability to meet the need for emerging skills, and, even more fundamentally, are not doing an adequate job of helping students learn how to learn and preparing them for a life where learning does not stop upon the awarding of a certificate or degree. And it's not just about helping students learn how to learn—we must also find ways to help them find and pursue a passion that will motivate them to learn throughout their lives.

If we pull back from all of these forces and contributing factors, we can capture the broader jobs challenge that we face as a global economy and society at two levels:

First, how can we ensure that we are all productively employed in ways that provide us with a rewarding living today? But, in a rapidly evolving world, that is only part of the challenge.

To really address the jobs challenge, we will need to focus on a second level as well: How do we redesign work so that it continues to challenge us to achieve and higher and higher levels of performance while providing us with the tools and environments required to realize more of our potential over time?

Another way of framing the jobs challenge at the highest level is to break it apart into three related dimensions:

- First, how do we create enough jobs to accommodate the growing segments of our population that want to or need to work?

- Second, how do we more effectively connect people seeking work with the available jobs where there is a good fit with their skills/interests?

- Finally, how do we ensure that we all are learning fast enough to enable us to continue to contribute effectively in a rapidly evolving work environment?

The bottom line is that we are facing a growing global disconnect between work that is available and rewarding, and people who need to and deserve to work.

Effectively addressing all dimensions of the jobs challenge will require significant and sustained innovation. We will not get to where we need to be simply by doing more of what we are doing today. We must go back to the basic assumptions that shape the institutions and practices driving our economy and society, and systematically challenge those assumptions in ways that generate a very different set of institutions and practices more capable of addressing the rapidly evolving needs of our workforce and our economy. The innovation that will matter the most here is institutional innovation—innovation that creatively reimagines the basic rationale of our institutions and designs an entirely new set of institutions and practices that can create growing value for participants.

Who Needs to be Involved?

Here's the problem: To address the jobs challenge effectively, we need an incredibly diverse set of stakeholders to innovate in fundamental ways.

In one dimension, we need companies—the primary drivers of job creation—to rethink how they define work. Today, most work is narrowly defined according to the activities that must be performed in a certain way within standardized and tightly integrated business processes. To thrive in an exponentially changing world, companies will need to redefine work in ways that encourage employees to accelerate the improvement of their performance and provide them with tools and platforms to develop more rapidly within the day-to-day work environment, rather than through the occasional training program. By redefining work in this way, companies will unleash the potential for growth in employment as they deliver more value to their markets. Rather than viewing workers as expense items to be cut and squeezed wherever possible, companies will start to see workers as resources capable of rapidly expanding value.

In parallel, technology and other forces are making it easier for people to seek productive work, not as employees of larger companies but as independent contractors or small teams in independent businesses. These work opportunities beyond the large corporation are in part enabled by services provided by larger businesses, ranging from job market platforms to back office services such as contract manufacturing or data processing services. The independent contractors and small teams will become even more productive and successful if they can find ways to learn faster by connecting with, and collaborating with, others in similar contexts.

In another dimension, we need schools to rethink their approach to education. Rather than viewing education largely as a transfer of pre-defined skills to new generations of students, schools will need to create innovative learning environments that will motivate students to learn faster and provide them with the tools they need to learn how to learn.

Governments are another key group of stakeholders. They will need to rethink all domains of public policy to accelerate the development of talent. This is not just about changing educational policy, but about systematically reassessing the impact of all public policy domains—e.g., immigration, intellectual property, urban policy, financial regulation, and business licensing—on talent development. More broadly, many governments will need to address the pervasive corruption and economic policies—e.g., regulations designed to prevent new entrants from challenging the entrenched positions of large, well-established firms—that contribute to economic stagnation and throttle back the pace and quality of job creation.

Let's not forget non-governmental organizations and other civic institutions. They can play a significant role in reaching out to marginalized portions of the population and helping them enter the workforce by giving them the tools and platforms they need to find meaningful and rewarding work.

And, at a completely different level, all of us as individuals who seeks to find and to pursue work that not only contributes to the institutions of which we are a part but also helps us to realize more of our own potential so that we can earn more and contribute more over time. A growing number of us who once viewed work simply as the source of a secure paycheck are now realizing that we need to take the initiative to develop our skills more rapidly if we are to remain competitive in a global labor market. This is becoming both an imperative and an opportunity for us to develop in ways that are more fulfilling.

All of these stakeholders have their own interests and agendas. The opportunity, and indeed the imperative, is to find ways to increase alignment of these interests and agendas around the shared goal of innovating for jobs.

The Ecosystem Imperative

Individual stakeholders can accomplish a lot on their own through their own initiative. But imagine how much more they could accomplish if they came together around shared goals and leveraged the diverse capabilities and resources of others.

Given the magnitude of the jobs challenge and the range of participants required to address it, an individual institution, no matter how large and well-positioned, will likely play only a small role in turning this challenge into an opportunity. We must find ways to bring a growing number of these stakeholders together in ways that can unleash increasing returns, so that the more participants who join in, the more rapidly and effectively we can innovate around new approaches to creating jobs that better develop our potential.

It is in this context that ecosystems will play a significant, and perhaps even critical, role in addressing the jobs challenge. Of course, all of these stakeholders already operate within existing ecosystems—no individual or institution is an island unto itself. Many of these ecosystems are emergent or self-organizing, having arisen spontaneously as individual participants found the need to interact with others in the economy and society.

What we are suggesting here is that there is an opportunity to create new ecosystems and to amplify the impact of existing ecosystems. In this context, we will focus on ecosystems that are intentional—that are designed by an organizer or orchestrator to bring diverse participants together to achieve shared goals. Of course, even intentional ecosystems have a significant component of spontaneous evolution as participants begin to interact with each other. One of the keys to the success of intentional ecosystems is for the organizer or orchestrator to strike the right balance between design and spontaneity.

These intentional ecosystems are typically driven by platforms—governance structures and a set of standards or protocols that help to facilitate interaction at scale among ecosystem participants. Properly designed, these ecosystems can dramatically amplify the efforts and resources of individual participants.

What kinds of ecosystem platforms might play a role in driving the proposed innovation for jobs narrative? There are at least four different types of platforms that could have significant impact in creating and scaling ecosystems to address this challenge:

- **Aggregation platforms.** These platforms focus on making resources conveniently accessible to participants. A classic example of this in the context of jobs would be a platform that more effectively matches job seekers and job creators, creating more transparent markets that align supply and demand. These platforms, such as Monster.com and Upwork, are typically hub and spoke models, in which all participants must go through a central facility to access the other side of a market. They also tend to be very transaction focused, matching a seeker with a supplier and typically collecting some kind of payment for having made the connection. The ecosystems created by these platforms can be very helpful in addressing part of the jobs challenge: giving job seekers a better view of jobs that might be appropriate for them.

- **Social platforms.** These platforms provide environments for participants to connect and get to know each other across the world, independent of space and time. Rather than facilitating transactions, these platforms have as their goal helping participants build lasting relationships and stay in touch with each other over time. These platforms seek to create increasingly rich networks where people can connect and have conversations around shared interests. In the context of the jobs challenge, these ecosystems become a key vehicle for helping job seekers and job creators alike recognize and explore shared interests. Rather than feeling isolated, participants begin to have a much richer awareness of others who have common interests and to build relationships that can give them even more sense of possibility and potential.

- **Mobilization platforms.** Now it starts to get really interesting. These platforms are explicitly designed to help participants come together and collaborate on a sustained basis on joint initiatives around shared goals. Classic examples of this kind of platform are open source initiatives, such as Linux, and efforts to orchestrate global supply networks, such as the one organized by Li & Fung in the apparel industry. Many different mobilization platforms might play a role in bringing together diverse stakeholders to address the jobs challenge. For example, imagine a mobilization ecosystem that seeks to bring together companies, non-governmental organizations, and government policy makers around shared initiatives within a country to create new jobs that more effectively address the evolving needs of the workforce. Another mobilization platform might bring together educational institutions to leverage each other's capabilities in innovating programs that accelerate learning and focus on teaching students to learn how to learn, rather than on transferring a specific set of knowledge or facts.

- **Learning platforms.** These are perhaps the ecosystems with the greatest impact of all. Rather than just trying to connect and mobilize existing capabilities and resources, these platforms are specifically designed to create environments that accelerate learning and performance improvement among the participants. They often do this by fostering the development of creation spaces—spaces designed to bring together small groups of people to help them build sustained and trust-based relationships around the shared goal of accelerating learning through action. Some of the most rapid and effective learning occurs in small, trust-based groups that enable participants to access and build upon each other's tacit knowledge—the knowledge that exists within each individual but is difficult for individuals to articulate to themselves, much less to others. By pursuing shared action in small groups, participants can learn from each other and rapidly refine their approaches to achieve even more impact.

The scaling of learning on these platforms occurs by connecting these small, action-oriented groups with each other through rich learning networks where they can observe the actions of other groups, ask questions across the groups, and share experiences more broadly. Again, in the context of the jobs challenge, imagine a job seeker learning ecosystem where job seekers connect with each other in small groups in their community to learn how to find appropriate jobs and then, once they have found jobs, continue to interact with each other to learn how to develop within their respective work environments. Or, imagine a government policy maker ecosystem that connects policy makers in small groups, perhaps within a single agency or a single state or province, to learn together how to craft and deploy public policies that will spur job creation and talent development of the workforce.

As a generalization, the first two types of ecosystems discussed above—aggregation and social—are really designed to increase the awareness of jobs in the current work environment and to improve the ability to act upon that awareness. This has significant value in its own right, because a large part of the jobs challenge today is the uneven distribution of information about the supply and demand of existing work. The innovation in these two ecosystems occurs at the ecosystem level, creating better platforms to increase the value that can be generated from the current work environment.

The second two types of ecosystems—mobilization and learn-ing—are designed to change the work environment through joint initiatives and learning that evolve both the supply (all of us as individuals) and the demand (all of the institutions seeking peo-ple to scale and perform their operations). This is potentially the most valuable innovation, because it aims to help all of us realize more of our potential by creating more opportunity, rather than by simply connecting existing supply with existing demand.

The really interesting opportunity is for these different types of ecosystems to evolve over time, refining and enhancing their plat-forms so they move from static transaction activity to dynamic, long-term relationships that foster more rapid learning and per-formance improvement. Rather than being mutually exclusive, ecosystems can evolve their platforms so they ultimately achieve all four of the goals outlined above: aggregating resources, build-ing meshed social networks, mobilizing participants on shared initiatives, and helping participants learn faster by working more closely together.

In the context of innovation for jobs, one of the most powerful attributes of ecosystems is that they productively integrate com-petition and collaboration, embodying the well-known concept of coopetition. At one level, all of the participants within an ecosys-tem have diverse interests and needs, and are likely to be pursu-ing initiatives that compete with those of other participants. Yet, at the same time, all of the participants are drawn together by the realization that they can accomplish a lot more through some form of collaboration. Because they have different backgrounds and perspectives, participants within an ecosystem are likely to disagree with each other, and there is often a lot of friction. But healthy ecosystems foster vigorous debate among participants but work to create an environment of mutual respect, so that these debates generate productive friction, leading to rich innovation and new insights and new approaches. Participants gain new in-sight not only by reflecting on their own experiences in the eco-system, but also by observing the actions of other participants and learning what works and what doesn't.

The Power of a Shared Narrative

While ecosystems can evolve and become increasingly useful to their participants, it would be unrealistic to expect a single ecosystem to be capable of tackling the jobs challenge. It is much more likely, and even desirable, that a growing number of focused ecosystems will emerge and evolve to address this challenge. Moreover, given their shared interests, it is likely that participants in these ecosystems will be involved in more than one ecosystem, and that the ecosystems themselves will begin to interact and build upon each other's initiatives in interesting and powerful ways. Ecosystems can interact in complex ways with an array of other ecosystems but retain their individual identities, just as the ecosystem "New York City" interacts with the financial services ecosystem but retains its own identity. The question will be how to foster these interactions so that the efforts within one ecosystem can build upon and amplify the learnings from other ecosystems.

In this context, it would help all of us to craft a shared narrative around innovation for jobs. What do I mean by this? I mean articulating and pursuing a shared view of the opportunity that cannot be achieved without the active participation of a growing number of individuals and institutions. Properly framed, narratives are a powerful call to action because they are open-ended and their resolution hinges upon the choices we make and the actions we take.

For these reasons, narratives are different from stories on two dimensions. Stories tend to be self-contained; they have a beginning, a middle, and an end, and something happens to resolve the story. Also, stories are typically about the storyteller or about some other group of people. They are not about you, the audience. The power of narratives derives from the fact that they are a call to action—they make it clear that whether the opportunity will be realized is up to us.

Narratives throughout history have played a powerful role in driving our political, social, and economic evolution. Think of the narrative that drove the Enlightenment: we are endowed with unique and extraordinary minds that are capable of enormous creativity and insight, but we all must make the effort to develop our minds and manifest that creativity through action, because the power of our minds is latent until we choose to develop it. An equally powerful narrative drove the growth and evolution of Silicon Valley: digital technology has the potential to change the world, but that potential can be realized only if you choose to move to Silicon Valley and join the effort to build new businesses that can change the world. Rich and rapidly evolving ecosystems emerged and expanded in response to these inspiring narratives.

Narratives have been powerful catalysts for intentional ecosystems, because they help us see a common opportunity that can be realized only if we come together and find ways to collaborate more effectively. Opportunity-based narratives are realistic about the challenges that must be faced and the obstacles that must be overcome in order to realize the opportunity, so they prepare us for the time and effort required to pursue the opportunity. At the same time, though, they help us magnify our perception of the reward that awaits us, while uniting us in the perception that we can overcome the risks if we come together. By fostering a shared commitment to a sustained effort to realize an opportunity, narratives help build long-term, trust-based relationships that are essential for high performing ecosystems. Since the opportunity expands as the number of participants increases, narratives also help to reduce the winner-take-all or zero-sum mindset that can quickly erode trust.

Our success in building rich and effective ecosystems that bring together diverse stakeholders around the opportunity of innovation for jobs will depend in part on our ability to craft a narrative that can capture the imagination and hearts of a growing number of participants. What might such a narrative look like?

A narrative doesn't just emerge from the pen of one person. But let me offer a flavor of what a narrative in this domain might look like. We live in a world that is increasingly shaped by exponential technologies that are spreading well beyond traditional computing into such diverse domains as 3D printing, biosynthesis, and energy. These technologies create both opportunities and challenges in terms of mounting performance pressure. Perhaps the biggest opportunity of all is to use these technologies as a catalyst to rethink work. We need to move beyond the conventional view of work as a set of pre-determined tasks that drove the Industrial Revolution. That outmoded model will lead to increasing automation and stress, and to a shrinking workforce.

Our opportunity now is to redefine work in ways that draw out what is uniquely human—creativity, imagination, emotional and social connection—to create far more value. We will then be in a position to harness all of this new technology to realize more of our potential as individuals and as organizations. But this opportunity requires us to challenge and to rethink virtually all of our current institutions and practices. There will be very strong resistance from those who cling to the past and fear the uncertainty of change. The opportunity will require each of us to venture beyond our comfort zones and to find ways to come together to develop the new practices and institutions required to support this very different view of work.

If we get this right, we will harness the potential of increasing returns and to create rapidly expanding economic value from the limited natural resources available to us. Rather than settling for sustainability, we will all benefit from thrivability, which will enable us to create increasing value with few resources and, in the process, to create new forms of work that are available not just for the privileged few, but for all of us. Rather than viewing the world as seven billion mouths to feed, we will be in a position to view it as seven billion minds to unleash.

That is just an example of an innovation for jobs narrative that could be a call to action and catalyst for the growth of the ecosystems needed to amplify our individual efforts. But narratives are not just words—they shape, and in turn are shaped by, action. They require role models who can communicate through their actions the opportunity to be realized. The key to evolving a successful narrative is to look for examples of initiatives that have already been undertaken and have already generated some impact consistent with the broader opportunity being framed. These examples then can become engaging stories to build credibility for the broader narrative. They also can shape the narrative as we develop more insight into what really is possible and what kinds of actions will be required to overcome the obstacles that stand between us and the opportunities ahead.

Successful narratives always strike a delicate balance between framing a compelling, long-term opportunity and focusing on near-term actions that people can take to start building impact and to strengthen the conviction that the longer-term opportunity is indeed achievable.

Innovation for jobs is a worthy challenge to pursue, but we will not realize its full potential—and even our very large institutions will not realize its full potential—unless we come together in broader and more diverse ecosystems that can leverage our individual efforts. Ecosystems are powerful drivers of distributed innovation that will help us discover new approaches that can help create work that is rewarding for everyone. Ecosystems take time to emerge and evolve, but we can focus on the power of narrative as a catalyst to accelerate the development of the ecosystems we will need for the journey ahead.

CHAPTER 4

Innovation Dynamics: Analytics Based on Big Data and Network Graph Science—Implications for Innovation for Jobs (i4j) Initiatives

By Daniel L. Harple, Jr.[1]

Abstract

This chapter describes big data and network graph analytics that can be used by i4j for mapping innovation for jobs ecosystems. The method discussed is called Pentalytics,[2] which derives

---

1   Daniel L. Harple is a co-chair of the i4j Analytics Special Interest Group, an MIT Sloan Fellow, an MIT Entrepreneur-in-Residence, and a visiting researcher at the MIT Media Lab. He is the Managing Director of Context Labs, and the Managing Partner of Shamrock Ventures, B.V., which is based in Amsterdam, The Netherlands, and Cambridge, Massachusetts. He has been a technology entrepreneur for twenty-five years, having founded and built technologies, companies, and products that have been used by billions of Internet users, innovating in Voice over IP (VoIP) & media streaming (InSoft/Netscape), Big Data (Context Media/Oracle Fusion), and location based social networking (gypsii/Sina Weibo). He is also a musician, sailor, and father of five children

   https://www.berklee.edu/people/dan-harple

   http://i4j.info/encyclopedia/dan-harple/

   http://www.media.mit.edu/research/groups/1458/measuring-urban-innovation

   https://www.linkedin.com/in/danharple

2   The Pentalytics sample size for the analysis in this chapter was 7,592 U.S.-based startups, a total of 908,007 people. A filter on software developers further downsized the sample to 54,500 people; 856 Boston-based job titles, 1,172 Silicon Valley job titles; 991 Boston-based firms, 1,468 Silicon Valley-based firms; 108 Boston-based industry segments, 131 Silicon Valley-based industry segments; 736 supply-chain universities to Boston-based firms, 1,500 supply-chain universities to Silicon Valley-based firms. Additional credit to Context Labs, specifically its Pentalytics R&D team: Daan Archer, Lee

an Innovation Cluster Density Index (ICDI) for a given location. The ICDI combines big data ingestion from disparate sources and network graph theory with descriptive and predictive algorithms to describe innovation clusters and ecosystems in new ways. ICDI outputs produce a variety of insights to help one better describe and predict innovation ecosystems. The ICDI outputs include urban innovation mappings, job requirements graphs, employee density maps by discipline, cluster heat maps, etc. The ICDI can compare ecosystems visually, for example, a biotech cluster in Cambridge with one in San Francisco. The ICDI platform, called InnovationScope (iScope) collects and ingests global innovation data in real time, around the clock, and provides a new and valuable tool to describe (and prescribe) an innovation for jobs framework. iScope can be used as an objective data-driven tool to further the i4j mission.

Innovation Dynamics

This chapter is based on work by the Context Labs team, the development of the MIT Sloan Regional Entrepreneurial Acceleration Lab program (REAL),[3] collaborations with MIT's Media Lab, and the development of big data/network graph Pentalytics,[4] with a platform called InnovationScope (iScope). In this chapter, it is discussed as a base for i4j Analytics to map and analyze innovation for jobs ecosystems. Innovation Dynamics is the implementation of Pentalytics, and applies a data-driven sensibility and vocabulary for the i4j agenda. The iScope platform enables stakeholders to contribute and run analytics models on their own, as well.

Innovation for jobs needs a language for discussing innovation dynamics. This new data-driven vocabulary can be then used to better understand how people, regions, states, and countries interact to maximize innovation and job creation. It is commonly

Harple, Gavin Nicol, Victor Kashirin.
3 The REAL program at MIT Sloan was founded by Dan Harple in 2012. http://real.mit.edu/
4 Harple, Daniel L. "Toward a Network Graph-Based Innovation Cluster Density Index," Massachusetts Institute of Technology, Sloan School of Management, 2013

believed that innovation happens in a small number of geo-graphical places, such as Silicon Valley. But in reality, innovation is people-centric and global. It is everywhere. If we are to spurn innovation for jobs globally, we need a better narrative for inno-vation ecosystems that pays attention to the global scale. The in-novation for jobs ecosystem is a global network of interconnected talent, resources, and innovative capacity. This is now described using Pentalytics, which derives an ICDI for a given geography, to deeply describe its innovative capacity in a variety of industry segments.

Innovation Ecosystems

Pentalytics uses algorithms and network graph theory to describe innovation by producing ecosystem graphs, with entities (nodes) that interact (described by edges connecting the nodes). With this approach, we can generate analytics for innovation for jobs that relate local and global conditions. We can measure the interaction between local actions and global trends. We can design analytics for global and local decision makers, enabling them to leverage on each other's decisions. An example is the deployment of innova-tion funding in the EU.[5] By better understanding the innovation clusters and their regions more deeply, policies and funding could be better targeted. The ICDI provides a deeper data-driven under-standing of the attributes needed for innovation and job creation. The diagram at right depicts the core elements and network flow permutations defining a Pentalytics model.

ICDI Pentalytics can be used in a variety of ways: (a) innovation for jobs experiments to seek and test driving factors, such as peo-ple, education, location amenities, funding, existing firms, etc. (b) a new vocabulary to describe innovation for jobs, the intercon-nected network effects, and the ways those drive job creation for cities, regions, countries (c) an economic cluster modeling and tracking tool (d) Innovation for jobs heat maps.

---

5 "Funding for Innovation - European Commission," http://ec.europa.eu/growth/industry/innovation/funding/index_en.htm.

Primary Pentalytic Elements

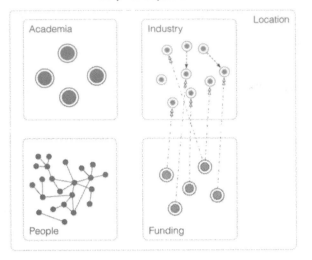

Innovation dynamics can be used for analyzing innovation eco-system resilience and failure. It can help make decisions for resource allocations, partnership and contractual targets, angel and venture funding strategies, and so on.

With data from social networks, geolocation, and mobility, innovation dynamics can map the history of the when, what, where, and who of an ecosystem. It can produce the analytics for grasping the why and the how, and for deciding the next and the when.

The present work we are undertaking can deepen the understanding of causality, enable diagnostics, and point toward prescriptive measures. Our aim is to provide diagnostics for cluster dynamics and economic expansion.

Innovation Clusters: The Context for Innovation Dynamics

Developing innovation dynamics requires a framework or context to help evaluate the diverse components necessary for innovation to flourish and to drive jobs. There are a variety of ways to describe innovation, and how it develops and breeds in clusters:

According to the U.S. Department of Commerce (2008), innovation is "the design, invention, development and/or implementation of new or altered products, services, processes, systems, organizational structures, or business models for the purpose of creating new value for customers and financial returns for the firm." Other authors offer similar definitions, including the Federal Reserve Bank of St. Louis (2007), which defines innovation as "taking something established and introducing a new idea, method or device that creates a new dimension of performance" and adding value."[6]

Further, contemporary clusters have tended to be researched and studied predominantly through the lens of Michael Porter's seminal 1990s work, "The Competitive Advantage of Nations-1998."[7] Implicit to the understanding of Porter's work is the much earlier work done in the early 1900s by Alfred Marshall, the founder of the Cambridge School of Economics. Marshall's work on agglomeration is the forefather of Porter's work, in that it touches on elements related to clusters, co-location of firms, and the advantages thereof. Carlson's definition[8] is distilled even more so, with a focus on the innovator and inventor: "Innovation is the creation and delivery of new customer value in the marketplace, with a sustainable business model."

One key takeaway from innovation dynamics research and big data platform development is that innovation thrives in clusters, not in isolation. This means that the media's overt focus on Silicon Valley as the tech industry one-and-only is not supported by the data.

---

6   Timothy Slaper and others, "The Index of Innovation: A New Tool for Regional Analysis," *Economic Development Quarterly* 25 (2011): 36–53

7   Michael E. Porter, *The Competitive Advantage of Nations* (New York: Free Press, 1990; republished with a new introduction, 1998).

8   Curt Carlson, "Definition of Innovation," *Practice of Innovation*, accessed August 25, 2015, http://www.practiceofinnovation.com/definition-of-innovation/. A founding member of i4j is Curtis R. Carlson, Ph.D., Founder and CEO, Practice of Innovation, Former President and CEO of SRI International, 1998–2014.

Innovation Everywhere

Innovation is everywhere; it just manifests itself in the context of its cluster density and innovative capacity. This new data-driven view from innovation dynamics yields a range of new network science-driven metrics for regions and cities. This means one can call out a location's innovative capacity, in terms of an innovation for jobs strategy. Each place has an Innovation Cluster Density Index (ICDI) for the market segment it supports. For example, Silicon Valley has a different ICDI for Internet, SaaS firms, semi-conductors, social, etc., with its supporting infrastructure (universities, firms, workforce, policies, sources of funding). And, each city around the world does as well. Using the Pentalytics dataset model, we now have a common and robust dataset, suitable for comparisons, interventions, prescriptions, and predictions. These new indices can help us decipher how and why different locations are more or less suitable for new innovation models. At the core of i4j, using this dataset and associated data-driven models, we can describe and prescribe, with much higher degrees of accuracy, where and what we can do for new innovation to drive jobs. This now provides a data-driven framework to inform policy, and funding. As an example, EU funding[9] for innovation is driven by strategic policy initiatives, and represents an extremely large opportunity for i4j impact, using Pentalytics-driven models.

It is clear that the network effects in Silicon Valley have worked so well that, to many people, innovation equates to Silicon Valley. In reality, this is not entirely the case. When you look more deeply you find that much of the innovation from Silicon Valley is actually outsourced to India, Eastern Europe, and other places. It does not fit the "we-are-the-best-and-brightest mantra" for Silicon Valley firms to tell customers that their coolest code was written by a team in Poland. Apple's "Designed by Apple in California" products are truly enabled by leveraging the advanced manufacturing

9   Over 76 percent of the EU budget is managed in partnership with national and regional authorities through a system of "shared management", largely through five big funds—the Structural & Investment Funds. Collectively, these help to implement the Europe 2020 strategy. http://europa.eu/about-eu/funding-grants/.

delivered by Foxconn in Shenzhen, China. This decoupling of cluster attributes is truly global, making it ever more critical for leaders to understand the global connectedness of their regions' ICDI attributes.

Innovation for Jobs Policy as a Data-driven Initiative

By talking about innovation as a global phenomenon, not as a Silicon Valley exclusive, i4j can do a service to the world. Pentalytics provides core ICDI data to support this view. The relationship of i4j with the Organization for Economic Co-operation and Development can help in this regard.

Using Pentalytics-driven ICDIs as a data-driven context, it is possible that the global government funding may be increased and better channeled to the right places. Without an ICDI to target investments, governments and policymakers essentially shoot into the dark. A data-driven model with i4j, using ICDI as key indicators, is a positive step to enhance and accelerate innovation and the creation of new jobs. The EU Budget for economic and innovation investment is in the hundreds of billions, as shown below, for years 2014 2020.[10] Clearly, using an ICDI tool to better aim and target investments in innovation would yield better results.

The Innovative Risk to Silicon Valley

The mechanics and inter-workings of Silicon Valley have been studied in depth and documented in a wide variety of books, journals, and media. The classic sociological paper, "The Role of Venture Capital Firms in Silicon Valley's Complex Innovation Network,"[11] by Michel Ferrary and Mark Granovetter, discusses at length innovative clusters and complex networks. Innovation dynamics and ICDI frameworks can be leveraged as tools for nav-

---

10 "Open Data Portal for the European Structural Investment Funds - European Commission," https://cohesiondata.ec.europa.eu/funds/erdf.

11 Michel Ferrary and Mark Granovetter, "The Role of Venture Capital Firms in Silicon Valley's Complex Innovation Network," *Economy and Society* 18 (May 2009): 326–359, https://sociology.stanford.edu/publications/role-venture-capital-firms-silicon-valleys-complex-innovation-network.

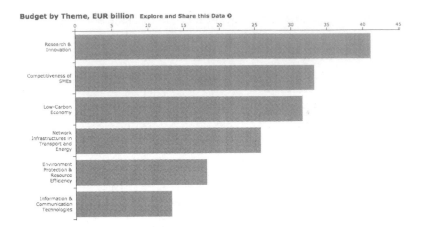

Budget by Theme, EUR billion Explore and Share this Data ⊙

igiting global innovation trends and optimizing Silicon Valley's resources, now and into the future.

The risk to Silicon Valley is that it is by nature an insular culture. Yet, the world has grown more inclusive, diverse, and distributed. As the Internet and Web are distributed and self-healing by design, Silicon Valley is centralized, less inclusive, and hardly global. Sand Hill Road as the Mecca of venture capital investing attests to this fact. Leading entrepreneurs in European startups are almost always told that they must relocate to Silicon Valley, in spite of the unique ecosystem attributes in their own backyards that caused them to innovate in the first place. This is a symptom of an innovation cancer recognized more than eighty years ago by Alfred Marshall. It represents a significant innovative risk to the sustainability of Silicon Valley in a global innovation-driven economy.

Marshall's work,[12] for all its groundbreaking depth and relevance, offers insights into not only the growth of clusters—i.e., "industrial districts"—but also their demise. This is relevant in that Michael Porter's work often is criticized for its lack of analysis of the actors in the economy, the actual people and entrepreneurs who are the real DNA for innovation and entrepreneurialism. Eighty years ago, Marshall spoke to the network effect of technology transfer in his explanation of the demise and collapse of various

12 Marshall, 1919.

British industrial districts.[13] A similar global risk exists for Silicon Valley and the American economy. An understanding of innovative cluster dynamics can be a strategic tool for avoiding this potentially devastating outcome.

Excessive clustering agglomeration has its downside. The not invented here (NIH) effects, which develop in Silicon Valley, are remarkably similar to the Marshallian observation of Victorian superiority. This has been documented as well in "Silicon Valley's 'One-hour' Distance Rule and Managing Return on Location," a paper by Griffith, Yam, and Subramaniam. These writers documented the positive impacts of geographical clusters, but also discussed a variety of downside effects as well.[14]

It is clear that an ICDI framework can help Silicon Valley not only sustain an edge and, therefore, ensure and grow jobs, but also target other regions and countries that will provide deep knowledge, invention, and innovation to accelerate growth and, therefore, jobs. This bodes well for the i4j economy.

---

13 See the discussion of Marshall's comments about the collapse of British industrial districts in the following section of this chapter, "Unicorn Mentality and Disruption Corruption."

14 "However, assessments also show a downside to the effects of geographical clustering. We believe there are three basic tensions. First, a concentration of economic activity will be followed by a concentration of labour and infrastructure (Zook, 2002). That can make the networks easier to manage (e.g, Owen-Smith and Powell, 2004), but may also create costs. In the recent boom period of Silicon Valley, the workforce gap (the gap between needed and available job candidates) was found to be around 39 percent. This gap resulted in incremental costs of $6 to $7 billion annually (Madan et al., 2002)—costs for moving people to the region, higher real estate costs, and cost of living. Second, group or innovation success relies in part on informational diversity (reviewed in Griffth and Neale, 2001). Organizations or networks reduce their diversity and possibly their long-term innovative capability when they draw from similar populations. There are benefits to networking diverse companies and cultures and yet clustering industries works against this. Third, some good prospect firms may simply not want to move." Griffith, T. L., P.J. Yam, and S. Subramaniam, "Silicon Valley's 'One-Hour' Distance Rule and Managing Return on Location," Venture Capital, 9, no. 2 (2007): 85–106. doi:10.1080/13691060601076202.

Unicorn Mentality and Disruption Corruption

The general public and tech press point to the current one percent Unicorn Club venture capital culture in Silicon Valley, a type of winner-take-all model that rewards valuation, not invention or innovation per se. A focus on this mode of operation defeats an i4j model, as it isolates attention and focus on small subsets of ICDI ecosystem firms (the "Unicorns). This, by nature, will tend to reduce the innovation need for <u>diverse</u> jobs, as the Unicorn investment thesis, in many ways, drives resource allocations in terms of hiring and new positions.

In a larger context, the Unicorn network effect may degrade the local and regional talent ecosystems by diverting jobs and hiring into a set of Unicorn firms that are not necessarily driven by economic output, but financial valuation. It has been shown that bubble mentality financing in the venture community has funded Unicorns with valuations that may never be realized by the firm's true economic output or production.[15] This is a known effect in systems dynamics modeling, as a negative reinforcing loop, or balancing loop, which can produce negative system outcomes.[16]

In a Pentalytics context, the "system" is the local or regional economy and its innovative capacity. A Unicorn-driven financing model, with its emphasis on valuation outcome often ignores a region's innate assets. Thus, the risk profile is increased for a region, i.e., Silicon Valley. Alfred Marshall's insights on agglomeration in the United Kingdom, circa 1919, speak to the way Victorian superiority ultimately led to its demise. The culture developing in Silicon Valley and San Francisco reinforces its own self-aggrandizement. This story has played out before. In the early 1920s, "the ill-conceived Victorian heredity of believing themselves technically superior to any international competitor, meant that local entrepreneurs missed the radical change of global competitive conditions whose consequence, in the absence of any positive reaction,

---

15 "Tech Startups Feel an IPO Chill—WSJ," http://www.wsj.com/articles/tech-startups-feel-an-ipo-chill-1445309822.

16 Jay W. Forrester et al., *MIT System Dynamics Group Literature Collection*, 2003.

was the unceasing collapse of the Lancashire district and of many British industrial districts."[17] Silicon Valley's use of i4j methods, data-driven by ICDI frameworks, may be a tool for avoiding the Unicorn trap.

The Unicorn mentality only reinforces a Valley-centric NIH, bolstered by a perverse drive toward disruption at all costs. The en vogue use of disruption does not necessarily reflect Clay Christensen's description, as it often appears as more of a destructive force for valuation gain than a value-add for society and the economy at large. As Christensen wrote in December 2015, "In our experience, too many people who speak of "disruption" have not read a serious book or article on the subject. Too frequently, they use the term loosely to invoke the concept of innovation in support of whatever it is they wish to do. Many researchers, writers, and consultants use "disruptive innovation" to describe *any* situation in which an industry is shaken up and previously successful incumbents stumble. But that's much too broad a usage."[18]

This is a place where an i4j innovation for jobs mission can also bolster Silicon Valley. Using a data-driven ICDI approach will help identify the broader range of entrepreneurial opportunities existing in an ecosystem. This can then minimize the shadow overhanging Unicorns, as it may drive resources (people, funding, intellectual property) to other innovation-driven efforts, thereby distributing the financial risk load to the ecosystem.

The i4j Agenda - Providing a Tangible Solution for Job Creation

Pentalytics-driven ICDI modeling also will allow us a more refined targeting of locations for new forms of employment. For example, one of the discoveries in our Pentalytics research about these innovation zones (clustered ecosystems) is the concept of

---

17 Fiorenza Belussi and Katia Caldari, "At the Origin of the Industrial District: Alfred Marshall and the Cambridge School," *Cambridge Journal of Economics* 33, no. 2 (2009): 335–355. doi:10.1093/cje/ben041.
18 "What Is Disruptive Innovation?," https://hbr.org/2015/12/what-is-disruptive-innovation.

innovative viscosity and/or fluidity. These are concepts that describe the innovative flow in an ecosystem. The flows of talent, intellectual property, funding, and infrastructure are all represented as ICDI metrics, providing a new lens through which to view innovative capacity and the ecosystems in which it thrives.

An i4j agenda can and should address these factors. As we better understand these types of innovation dynamics, we can further the i4j goal to catalyze innovation for new and highly productive sustaining jobs, and not just drive investment for destructive disruption and short term valuation exit opportunities.

Early Pentalytics ICDI Analytics—Snapshot Visualization Examples

ICDI analytics are providing new insights into innovation, innovation for jobs, and the way a region's economic and strategic innovation assets describe innovative capacity. This chapter is intended as an overview into the Pentalytics framework, its technology implementation with InnovationScope, for its application in i4j's initiatives.

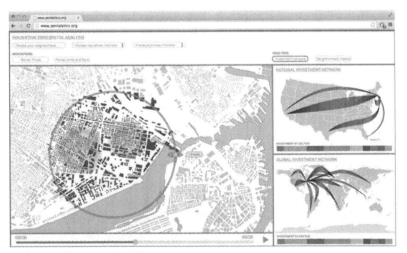

Figure 1: Innovative Capacity Spatial Analysis Browser

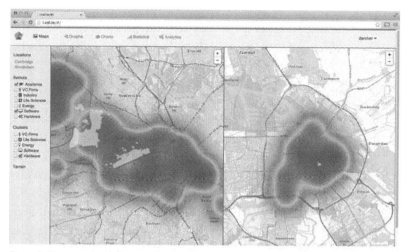

Figure 2: Comparative Adjacency Browser

The following graphics depict early examples of ICDI Analytics and provide a snapshot of the utility and versatility of this new technology tool.

InnovationScope (iScope) enables comparative geographical visualizations illustrating a wide range of factors: investment network flow, industry segment flow, innovative viscosity, etc. Note that unlike most map-based visualizations, Pentalytics, driven by network science methods, also provides insights into flow between elements (edges), and not just the elements (nodes). The example below focuses on Cambridge and MIT:

IScope enables visual side-by-side comparisons that display heat maps describing company sectors, employee resources, and ame nities presented as geographical adjacencies. This informs the relationship between local academic institutions and technology sectors—e.g., Cambridge vs. Amsterdam.

The example below provdes a side-by-side visualization examining the proximity relationships anchored by the pentalytic component of Academia, illustrating the adjacent innovations and industry segment firms surrounds an academic geolocation. This example considers Cambridge on the left, showing Harvard and

MIT primarily, and Amsterdam on the right, focusing on the University of Amsterdam:

A variety of side-by-side comparisons can be visualized. For example, one could consider the people resources by skill type in evaluating an industry, e.g., Biotech, and comparing this element from one geolocation to another. This means if one were to consider funding into the acceleration of a strategic Biotech cluster or region, the sources of talent would be now visualized as key indicators of success. In this regard, all Pentalytics attributes and variables can be packaged into unique visualizations, dependent on the desired insight. Further, the toolset can be leveraged to also inform where new locations exist which needs a specific type of skill. In this view, gaps in a cluster can then be viewed as new opportunities for job creation, and inform the movement of talent from one location to another.

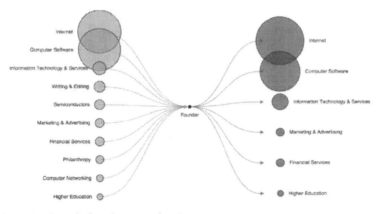

Figure 3: Where do founders come from?

As new companies are formed, clearly, new jobs are formed. With that, a key premise of innovation for jobs is to accelerate the creation of new firms. A catalyst for the founding of new firms is the acceleration of the development of innovative founders, their skill sets, their backgrounds, optimizing in their locations. Our work has preliminarily given us some inputs on where founders come from, and what specific "innovation everywhere" location attributes spawn them.

Figure 3, below, illustrates the industry flow for individuals in the Silicon Valley/San Francisco Internet cluster who identify themselves as founders. Note that the top three sectors—Internet, Computer Software, and IT/Services—are on both the "From" and "To" sides of the graph. Interestingly, the next "supply-side" industry for a founder in this innovation geo-cluster comes from Writing and Editing, Semiconductors, Marketing and Advertising, etc. The nodes in the graph are sorted by magnitude of job titles. This insight also makes a case for a liberal arts education, as the ability to write and edit is now proven with data-driven analytics, as a key attribute for being a company founder.

The data analytics in the Figure 3 scenario illustrate that:

- Founders flow between industry sectors.
- Founders have a high degree of inter-sector networking.
- Industry flow shows migration from sector to sector.
- Founders produce quality jobs fast.
- Founders had less senior roles in their originating companies.
- Most founders come from adjacent sector firms.

For Silicon Valley, the data analytics also reveal that founders come primarily from seventy-one academic institutions and ten predominant industry segments, and become founders from a top core of eighteen specific job titles.

From a university perspective, the top suppliers of Internet segment Silicon Valley founders are as follows, with part of the long-tail shown as well:

- Stanford dominates among those identifying as founders and co-founders
- University of California, Berkeley
- Massachusetts Institute of Technology
- University of California, Davis

- San Jose State University

- University of California, Los Angeles

- University of California, Santa Barbara

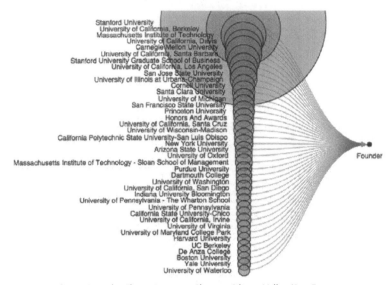

Figure 4: Academia Founder Flow - Internet Cluster- Silicon Valley/San Francisco

References

Archibugi, Daniele, Mario Denni, and Andrea Filippetti, "The Technological Capabilities of Nations: The State of the Art of Synthetic Indicators," Technological Forecasting and Social Change 76, no. 7 (2009): 917–931, doi:10.1016/j. techfore.2009.01.002.

Becker, Gary S., "Investment in Human Capital: A Theoretical Analysis," Journal of Political Economy 70, no. 5 (1962): 9–49, doi:10.2307/1829103.

Bell, Geoffrey G., "Clusters, Networks, and Firm Innovativeness. Strategic Management Journal 26, no. 3 (2005): 287-295, doi:10.1002/smj.448.

Belussi, Fiorenza, and Katia Caldari, "At the Origin of the Industrial District: Alfred Marshall and the Cambridge School,"

Cambridge Journal of Economics 33, no. 2 (2009): 335–355, doi:10.1093/cje/ben041.

Bresnahan, Timothy, Alfonso Gambardella, and Annalee Saxenian, "'Old Economy' Inputs for 'New Economy' Outcomes: Cluster Formation in the New Silicon Valleys," Industrial and Corporate Change 10, no. 4 (2001): 835.

Carlson, Curt, "Definition of Innovation," Practice of Innovation, accessed August 25, 2015, http://www.practiceofinnovation.com/definition-of-innovation/.

Christensen, Clay. "What Is Disruptive Innovation?" *Harvard Business Review*, no. December 2015. https://hbr.org/2015/12/what-is-disruptive-innovation.

Delgado, Mercedes, Christian Ketels, Michael E. Porter, and Scott Stern, "The Determinants of National Competitiveness," National Bureau of Economic Research (2012). Retrieved from http://www.frdelpino.es/wp-content/uploads/2012/11/DKPS_w18249.pdf.

Delgado, Mercedes, Michael E. Porter, and Scott Stern, "Clusters and Entrepreneurship," Journal of Economic Geography 10, no. 4 (2010): 495–518.

Demaine, Erik D., Dotan Emanuel, Amos Fiat, and Nicole Immorlica, "Correlation Clustering in General Weighted Graphs," Theoretical Computer Science 361, nos. 2–3 (2006): 172–187, doi:10.1016/j.tcs.2006.05.008.

Drucker, Peter F., "The Discipline of Innovation," Harvard Business Review 76, no. 6 (1998): 149–157.

Eesley, Charles. E., and William F. Miller, "Impact: Stanford University's Economic Impact via Innovation and Entrepreneurship," Stanford University (October 2012), http://engineering.stanford.edu/sites/default/files/Stanford_Alumni_Innovation_Survey_Report_102412_1.pdf.

Etzkowitz, Henry, and Loet Leydesdorff, "The Dynamics of Innovation: From National Systems and 'Mode 2' to a Triple Helix of

University-Industry-Government Relations," Research Policy 29, no. 2 (2000): 109–123, doi:10.1016/S0048-7333(99)00055-4.

Feldman, Maryann P., and Richard Florida, "The Geographic Sources of Innovation: Technological Infrastructure and Product Innovation in the United States," Annals of the Association of American Geographers 84, no. 2 (1994): 210–229, doi:10.1111/j.1467-8306.1994.tb01735.x.

Ferrary, Michel, and Mark Granovetter, "The Role of Venture Capital Firms in Silicon Valley's Complex Innovation Network," Economy and Society 38, no. 2 (2009): 326—359, doi:http://dx.doi.org/10.1080/03085140902786827.

Forrester, Jay W., System Dynamics Society, Sloan School of Management., and System Dynamics Group. MIT System Dynamics Group Literature Collection, 2003.

Funding for Innovation - European Commission." Accessed January 9, 2016. http://ec.europa.eu/growth/industry/innovation/funding/index_en.htm.

Furman, Jeffrey L., Porter, Michael. E., and Scott Stern, "The Determinants of National Innovative Capacity," Research Policy 31, no. 6 (2002): 899–933.

Global Innovation Index, http://www.globalinnovationindex.org/content/page/GII-Home (retrieved April 16, 2013).

Griffith, Terri L., Patrick J. Yam, and Suresh Subramaniam, "Silicon Valley's 'One-Hour' Distance Rule and Managing Return on Location," Venture Capital 9, no. 2 (2007): 85–106, doi:10.1080/13691060601076202.

Harple, Daniel L., "Toward a Network Graph-Based Innovation Cluster Density Index," Massachusetts Institute of Technology, Sloan School of Management, 2013.

Hidalgo, César, Ricardo Hausmann, and Partha Sarathi Dasgupta, ed., "The Building Blocks of Economic Complexity," Proceedings of the National Academy of Sciences of the United States of America 106, no. 26 (2009): 10570–10575, doi:10.2307/40483593.

Kunegis, Jérôme, "Why Everything is a Network," Network Science (November 11, 2011), http://networkscience.wordpress.com/2011/11/21/why-everything-is-a-network/ .

Marshall, Alfred, Industry and Trade (London: Macmillan, 1919).

Owen-Smith, Jason, and Walter W. Powell, "Knowledge Networks as Channels and Conduits: The Effects of Spillovers in the Boston Biotechnology Community," Organization Science 15, no. 1 (2004): 5–21, doi:10.1287/orsc.1030.0054.

Padgett, John F., and Christopher K. Ansell, "Robust Action and the Rise of the Medici," American Journal of Sociology 98, no. 6 (1993): 1259–1319.

Porter, Michael E., The Competitive Advantage of Nations: With a New Introduction. (New York: Free, 1998).

Porter, Michael E., "The Five Competitive Forces that Shape Strategy," Harvard Business Review 86, no. 1 (January 2008): 79–93+137.

Porter, Michael. E., Mercedes Delgado, Christian Ketels, and Scott Stern, "Moving to a New Global Competitiveness Index," Global Competitiveness Report 2008-2009 (2008): 43–63.

Powell, Walter (Woody) W., Kelley A. Packalen, and Kjersten Bunker Whittington, "Organizational and Institutional Genesis: The Emergence of High-Tech Clusters in the Life Sciences," SSRN Scholarly Paper No. ID 1416306, Rochester, New York: Social Science Research Network (2010). Retrieved from http://papers.ssrn.com/abstract=1416306.

Roberts, Edward B., and Charles E. Eesley, "Entrepreneurial Impact: The Role of MIT—An Updated Report," Foundations and Trends in Entrepreneurship 7, nos. 1-2 (2011): 1–149.

Saxenian, Annalee, "[Review of] Engines of Enterprise: An Economic History of New England," The Journal of Economic History 63, no. 3 (September 2003): 905–906.

Saxenian, Annalee, "Silicon Valley's New Immigrant High-Growth Entrepreneurs," Economic Development Quarterly 16, no. 1 (2002): 20–31.

Winkler, Rolfe, Douglas Macmillan, Telis Demos, and Monica Langley. "Tech Startups Feel an IPO Chill - WSJ." Wall Street Journal, October 19, 2015, sec. Tech. http://www.wsj.com/articles/tech-startups-feel-an-ipo-chill-1445309822.

CHAPTER 5

Accelerating Toward a Jobless Future: The Rise of the Machine and the Human Quest for Meaningful Work

By Steve Jurvetson and Mo Islam[1]

Abstract

The future will present a new paradigm in master and slave: the slaves of the future will be our machines. We will have automated all work, including engineering, diagnosis of diseases, and discovery of new scientific principles. The driver of these feats of innovation will continue to be Moore's Law, the model that explains how humanity's capacity to compute has been compounding continuously. The combinatorial explosion of possible idea pairings will grow exponentially as new ideas come into the mix, as dictated by Reed's Law, and will further increase economic growth and accelerate technological change. One of the first substantial job displacements caused by accelerating innovation will be seen in the self-driving car. Ultimately, there won't be jobs for humans in the sense we think of today. Instead, we will have to pursue meaning and purpose through other means, whether hobbies or entertainment, in order to sustain a thriving civilization.

---

1 Steve Jurvetson is a partner at DFJ and Mohammad Islam is an associate at DJF.

A New Paradigm

Let's go far enough in the future where no one will debate the sweeping transition of time. There are infinite possible paths to this distant future, but we can imagine reasonable endpoints. This future will look like much of human history prior to the industrial and agricultural revolutions, where serfs and slaves did most of the labor-intensive work in the city-state economies. But while we hope the arc of the moral universe continues to bend towards justice, there will be a new paradigm in master and slave relationship between man and his machine. The slaves of the future will be our machines.

There won't be many jobs in the sense that we think of them for most people today. Machines will take over mechanically repetitive tasks. Humans will ever only need to do this type of work if they choose to, but they will not provide the most efficient means to complete these tasks. Even highly skilled workers, such as engineers, doctors, and scientists, will have their professions disrupted by automation and artificial intelligence. We will automate engineering, we will automate diagnosis, and we will automate discovery of scientific principles. In this future, where the marginal cost of labor is zero and where companies have reached new bounds of profit maximization, both the microeconomics of individual companies and the macroeconomics of the global economy will be completely upended. Maslow's hierarchy of needs—food, shelter, health care, education—will be free for everyone forever. We won't need to work to achieve the basic building blocks of sustainable civilization. The only important human need that will be amplified in this distant future even more than it is now is the desire for meaning.

Humanity's Compounding Capacity to Compute

First, we will lay a framework for understanding why we believe this is a possible future. We are already on the trajectory to get us there—we have been since the dawn of the industrial age. Humanity's capacity to compute has been constantly compounding.

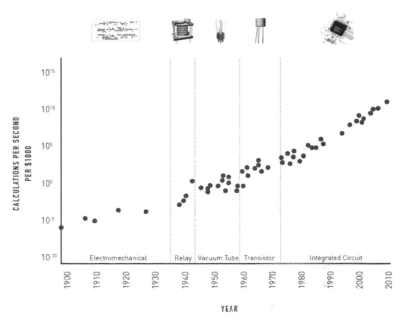

Figure 1: Ray Kurzweil's abstraction of Moore's Law. Each dot is a computer.

Incredibly, it can be explained through a simple and elegant model that, at first glance, may seem narrow in its explanatory power, but that tells a much deeper story. That model to describe this macrotrend begins with Moore's Law. Moore's Law is commonly reported as a doubling of transistor density every eighteen months. But unless you work for a chip company and focus on fab-yield optimization, you do not care about the transistor counts that Gordon Moore originally wrote about. When recast as a computational capability, Moore's Law is no longer a transistor centric metric.

What Moore observed in the belly of the early integrated circuit industry was a derivative metric, a refraction of a longer-term trend, a trend that begs various philosophical questions and predicts mind-bending futures. Ray Kurzweil's abstraction of Moore's Law[2] shows computational power on a logarithmic scale

---

2   Ray Kurzweil, "Exponential Growth of Computing," Kurzweil Accelerating Intelligence (April 9, 2010), http://www.kurzweilai.net/exponential-growth-of-computing Reprinted with permission.

and finds a double exponential curve that holds over 110 years! A straight line would represent a geometrically compounding curve of progress.

Through five paradigm shifts—such as electromechanical calculators and vacuum tube computers—the computational power that $1,000 buys has doubled every two years. For the past thirty years, it has been doubling every year.

Each dot is the frontier of computational price performance of the day. One machine was used in the 1890 census; one cracked the Nazi Enigma cipher in World War II; one predicted Eisenhower's win in the 1956 presidential election. Many of them can be seen in the Computer History Museum. Each dot represents a human drama. Prior to Moore's seminal paper in 1965, which presented what later became known as Moore's Law, none of them even knew they were on a predictive curve. Each dot represents an attempt to build the best computer with the tools of the day. Of course, we use these computers to make better design software and manufacturing control algorithms. And so the progress continues.

Notice also that the pace of innovation is exogenous to the economy. The Great Depression and the world wars and various recessions do not introduce a meaningful change in the long-term trajectory of Moore's Law. Certainly, the adoption rates, revenues, profits, and economic fates of the computer companies behind the various dots on the graph may go through wild oscillations, but the long-term trend emerges nevertheless.

In the modern era of accelerating change in the tech industry, it is hard to find even five-year trends with any predictive value, let alone trends that span the centuries. We would go further and assert that this is the most important graph ever conceived, and this is why it is so important as a foundation for understanding the future. We humans, regardless of external factors such as war, disease, and failing economies, have over vast periods of time doubled our capabilities to produce new technologies to propel us forward.

Accelerating Technological Progress

Moore's law has set the bar for the accelerating pace of computation and innovation. How can we expect it to keep accelerating to get even faster now to the distant future we describe? All new technologies are combinations of technologies that already exist. Innovation does not occur in a vacuum; it is a combination of ideas from before. In any academic field, the advances today are built on a large edifice of history. This is why major innovations tend to be "ripe" and tend to be discovered at nearly the same time by multiple people. The compounding of ideas is the foundation of progress, something that was not so evident to the casual observer before the age of science. Science tuned the process parameters for innovation and became the best method for a culture to learn.

From this conceptual base comes the origin of economic growth and acceleration of technological change, as the combinatorial explosion of possible idea pairings grows exponentially as new ideas come into the mix, as dictated by Reed's Law.[3] It explains the innovative power of urbanization and networked globalization. And it explains why interdisciplinary ideas are so powerfully disruptive; it is like the differential immunity of epidemiology, whereby islands of cognitive isolation (e.g., academic disciplines) are vulnerable to disruptive memes hopping across them, in much the same way that South America was vulnerable to smallpox from Cortés and the Conquistadors. If disruption is what you seek, cognitive island hopping is good place to start, mining the interstices between academic disciplines.

It is the combinatorial explosion of possible innovation-pairings that creates economic growth, and it is about to go into overdrive. In recent years, we have begun to see the global innovation effects of a new factor: the Internet. People can exchange ideas as never before. Long ago, people were not communicating across continents; ideas were partitioned, and so the success of nations

---

3   Reed's Law states that the utility of large networks, especially social networks, scales exponentially with the size of the network. The number of possible sub-groups of network participants n is 2^n. Thus, the value of the group-forming network increases exponentially.

and regions pivoted on their own innovations. Richard Dawkins states that in biology it is genes which really matter, and we as people are just vessels for the conveyance of genes.[4] It is the same with ideas or "memes." We are the vessels that hold and communicate ideas, and now that pool of ideas percolates on a global basis more rapidly than ever before.

Rise of the Machines

Moore's Law provides the model for us to understand humanity's continuous compounding capacity to compute—with that we have accelerating technological progress driven by the combinatorial explosion of new ideas by ever-increasing sub-groups of cognitively diverse people becoming connected. However, the ramifications of this longer-term trend will start to become apparent in the very short term. We believe the greatest disruptor for job displacement caused by this accelerating innovation is the self-driving car.

Automotive original equipment manufacturers and new companies are investing massive amounts of capital and engineering manpower to get to market with fully (Level 4) autonomous cars. The commercialization path of these self-driving cars, whether through an Uber-like on-demand service or through direct sales to consumers, is less important than the enormous impact they will have on the global job market. Using global employment data from the International Labour Organization (ILO),[5] we find that by 2019, 5.7 percent of global employment will be in the transport, storage, and communication sector (See Figure 2).[6] Moreover, the distribution of employment status data shows us that globally more than 60 percent of all workers lack any kind of employment

---

4   "The Selfish Gene," *Wikipedia*, http://en.wikipedia.org/wiki/The_Selfish_Gene.

5

6   Transport, storage, and communication include activities related to providing passenger or freight transport, whether scheduled or not, by rail, road, water, or air, and auxiliary activities, such as terminal and parking facilities, cargo handling, and storage. Division 64 includes postal activities and telecommunications. In particular, the renting of transport equipment with driver or operator for each of the different transport modes is considered to be a transport activity and is therefore included in this section.

contract, with most of them engaged in unpaid or family work in the developing world (See Figure 3). We find that, of workers worldwide who have paid full-time jobs (excluding temporary workers), almost 20 percent drive as their form of employment today!

And autonomous vehicles are only the tip of the iceberg. As these systems transcend human comprehension, we will shift from traditional engineering to evolutionary algorithms and iterative learning algorithms such as deep learning and machine learning. While these techniques are powerful, the locus of learning shifts from the artifacts themselves to the process that created them. The beauty of compounding iterative algorithms (evolution, fractals, organic growth, art) derives from their irreducibility. And it empowers us to design complex systems that exceed human understanding, which we increasingly need to do at the cutting edge of software engineering. This process presents a plausible path to general artificial intelligence, or what Ray Kurzweil and others refer to as "strong A.I." Danny Hillis summarizes succinctly in

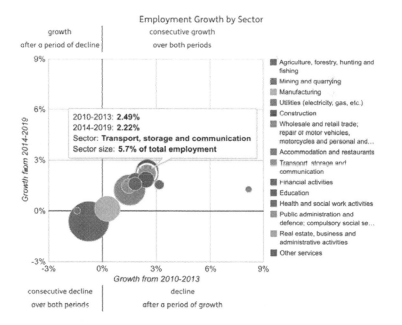

Figure 2: Employment growth by sector, in which transport is one of the fasting growing.

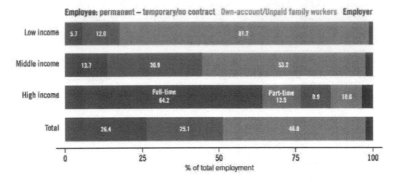

Figure 3: Distribution of employment status, showing that only 40 percent of people have full-time jobs

the conclusion from his programming primer *The Pattern on the Stone*: "We will not engineer an artificial intelligence; rather we will set up the right conditions under which an intelligence can emerge. The greatest achievement of our technology may well be creation of tools that allow us to go *beyond* engineering—that allow us to create more than we can understand." Once we build these systems that surpass human understanding and that may even surpass human intelligence, the number of jobs that will be overhauled is unbounded—leading us to a future where no one will have to work.

Meaningful Work

Moore's Law will drive human innovation forward and the collective global intelligence will create new forms of super artificial intelligence that can surpass human capabilities. This will completely disrupt our notion of jobs. Work is now the very thing that powers our global economy. But what happens when it no longer has to? Or at least, when most humans are no longer the aggregate primary drivers of global work, how will we find meaning in our lives? This existential phenomenon is one that will completely turn the current debate about the race against the machine on its head: the debate will no longer be about machines taking human jobs but instead about humans needing meaning in their work, even though it may no longer be for employment. The nature of jobs as we think about them today will dramatically change in the future, but humans will retain their thirst for deriving purpose from their actions. This is already becoming a major focus for employers now, as millennials entering the job market are interested in more than just salary, benefits, and job security to satisfy their work expectations.[7] They want to be a part of something larger, to fulfill a mission that can really change the world. As we look to this distant future where employment isn't necessary for most humans, finding meaning through non-traditional forms of work, whether hobbies, research, or entertainment will become paramount to sustaining a thriving civilization.

---

7   Karl Moore and Sienna Zampino, "Millennials Work for Purpose, Not Paycheck," *Forbes* (October 2, 2014), http://www.forbes.com/sites/karlmoore/2014/10/02/millennials-work-for-purpose-not-paycheck/.

CHAPTER 6

How to Disrupt Unemployment Policy?

By Sven Littorin[1]

When I resigned as the Minister for Employment after four years in 2010, I was the longest serving labor minister of all of the twenty-seven in the entire European Union. I was the second longest serving in my position in Swedish history. I would see ministers come and go at our Council of Ministers meetings in Brussels, evermore gloomy and hollow-eyed. And I could see myself getting less and less enthusiastic and visionary, and more tired and disillusioned as the days and months passed.

I can see why. In fact, I was not the Minister for Employment; I was the Minister of Unemployment. I had a budget of some 15 billion dollars, which is huge in a small country like Sweden. I had tens of thousands of people working in the authorities reporting to my ministry. And yet, almost every single program, grant, activity, or policy was focused not on anything close to creating jobs. Each and every tool in my toolbox was focused on cleaning up the mess when structural changes, business cycle hiccups, or plain and simple financial crises hit and created havoc in our economies.

This fundamental flaw in policy is not just a Swedish or European phenomenon. I saw the same thing in almost every ministry and country I had a chance to visit and every economy I had a chance

---

1 Sven Littorin is a co-founder of i4j, CEO of Serio and served as Sweden's Minister for Employment from 2006 to 2010.

to learn more about. It was certainly not the intention of the government I served in; on the contrary, even my title was changed from Minister *of* Labor to Minister *for* Employment to show the fundamental shift in focus from administering programs to actively pursuing a growing economy in which people had jobs. The "work first principle" was paramount to us, and every policy we designed was measured against its propensity to lower thresholds for people entering or coming back to the labor market.

It worked very well in most respects. In 2008, we could boast the fastest-falling unemployment rate among the all thirty-four member states of the Organization for Economic Cooperation and Development (OECD). We had record numbers of hours worked in the economy, and labor participation rates were at all-time high while labor market exclusion from unemployment, long-term sick leave, early retirement, and disability pension was on the decline. Even during and after the financial crisis in 2008-09, the Swedish economy was the star of the EU.

In its economic survey of Sweden in 2011, the OECD writes, "Sweden has weathered the recent global financial and economic crisis well thanks to strong economic institutions and fundamentals, not least a sound fiscal position.... Past reforms and measures taken during the crisis have limited the fall in employment and exits from the labour market."[2]

But being best in class when everyone else is lousy is not good enough. This is especially true as the fundamentals of economies change. The digitalization of our societies, which will increase the number of connected devices from 11 billion to 500 billion in fifteen years, will to my mind completely change the way we have to think and act when it comes to jobs in the future. To paraphrase the saying "The king is dead, long live the king!" I believe we have to get accustomed to the fact that "The job is dead, long live work!"

---

2   Organization for Economic Cooperation and Development, *OECD Economic Surveys: Sweden 2011* (OECD Publishing, January 2011), 8, http://dx.doi.org/10.1787/eco_surveys-swe-2011-en.

We can argue over exactly what is happening in the economy these days, but I am confident that one megatrend that is emeging is that fewer and fewer ordinary jobs will be needed to produce the same things we have become used to consuming. Let me cite one simple example. There were significant barriers of entry to produce little yellow rubber ducks in the traditional economy. You needed an expensive industrial mold; you needed plastic and color; you needed some proprietary product research, design, marketing, warehouses, logistics, sales people, and after-sales reps; and you needed a factory, printed business cards, a company car, and a corner office for the CEO. Today, you need a 3-D printer and a website—that's it.

Changes in technology have made it possible, with almost no investment, to customize very small series of products and make them immediately profitable. Researchers call it "the long tail," a democratization of production.

Another example: I know a young woman in the north of Sweden whose main interest is hair extensions. She started a blog about her interest, and subsequently began importing hair extensions and selling them to her friends and readers. Today, eight years on, her company Rapunzel has a turnover of close to $15 million. She certainly did not start and develop her company by the book; there was no research department, no marketing department, and no linear value chain. She created the company together with her "co-customers" who became the best sales force possible—a crowd of fans sharing an interest. This is an example of the individualization of demand.

Such changes are certainly not confined to traditional manufacturing jobs. Mobile health solutions are already changing the way health care is delivered. In Sweden, there is a project that equips scales with a mobile device so that heart patients can weigh in from home when calibrating their medicines, rather than having to go to the hospital to do so. In the short term, a project like this will free up time for nurses and doctors to focus on patients in need of hands-on care, but, let's face it, in the long run developments such as these are surely a road to fewer traditional jobs in this sector.

The gamification of education is another example. A few years ago, when I took my then thirteen-year-old son to Rome to see the sights, I was astonished to find that he knew more about the churches and palaces than I did, even though I am quite the history buff. The explanation was simple: he was an avid player of the video game *Assassin's Creed*, and the latest release at the time was set in medieval Rome and offered a fantastically detailed and historically accurate representation of the environment in which the game is set. No boring, old school history lesson on earth could have taught him as much as he learned from playing this game.

I am a resolute optimist about these technological developments; I believe they will broaden our horizons, make services and knowledge more accessible and cheaper, and make life easier and happier for our citizens. But they also pose a great challenge. When I consider the emergence of the new "nerdonomics," combined with ever increasing automation and digitalization, I can appreciate reports that predict that as many as 40 percent of today's jobs will disappear in the years to come.

So, are these trends of concern to policy makers today? No. I would say that most labor market policy makers around the globe have no clue whatsoever about these trends. And even if they did, their policy measures would be completely useless. How do you manage a structural change of this magnitude within todays' prevailing systems and theories? Better public employment services? Better functioning unemployment insurance systems? A tax deduction? A subsidy? Rubbish. We have to rethink and deconstruct most of what we know about labor market policy making to fit a future that is coming faster than we could ever predict.

Can this be done within the system? No. I would argue that the silos of government and the iron triangles outside them are too strong.

In any organization of some age and importance, there are hierarchies to match. Governments are as old as organizations get, and they work with a monopoly on violence and, in the best of cases, under the rule of law. Governments *should* be conservative (and to my mind Conservative, but that's another matter!). Why? Because governments without some vision, grace, and hesitance in lawmaking are mere hordes of populist spenders, regardless of political affiliation. Governments should think more about the long-term effects of their policies and less about their short-term appearances.

When translated into the operations of nations, this means governments are organized in very strong hierarchical pyramids with the president or prime minister at the top. Immediately below there are ministers and ministries, each with its own responsibilities and agenda. Below them are agencies and civil servants. The world outside is organized in much the same way; companies have divisions and subsidiaries, and newspapers and media outlets have editions and beats.

Now, a new economic order will transform the way companies and media houses have to work or they will go under. Social media have already put a lot of traditional papers out of business, and companies work every day to avoid the Kodak example of missing out on what is going on.

But we *will* have a government, like it or not. And governments have yet to show their willingness to change. Not even extremely low approval rates or election participation rates seem to do the trick.

One reason for this has to do with the old Churchillian proverb: "Democracy is the worst form of Government except for all those other forms that have been tried from time to time." We simply don't know any better alternative to today's hierarchical pyramids when it comes to governing a country.

Yet, governments have been exceptionally bad at addressing issues that cut across some of its own silos. Innovation is a prime example. Is innovation a matter for the educational system? Yes and no. Is it a matter for those involved in enterprise and industrial policies? Yes and no. Is it a matter for the treasury? Yes and no. So, if you were the president or prime minister, whom would you put in charge? What budgets should you allocate? And what policies would you pursue?

In addition, the future beyond the present election term is always very tricky for politicians. And when it comes to innovation and its effects on the labor market, we know surprisingly little as to the cause and effects of alternative policies.

We know that innovation explains three-quarters of growth over time, but we don't know which policy mix would speed up the way innovation turns into new jobs, and we don't know much about why and how innovation could or should assist in job growth rather than productivity growth.

A mix of policy lag, lack of research, and uncertainty over outcome in a very hierarchical and shortsighted system has driven innovation to pay lip service to the political system and no more. And no wonder. Had I gone to the Minister of Finance in Stockholm and asked him for a billion more for "innovation for jobs projects," he would have laughed at me and made me walk back to my hole in the ground in shame. Why? Because he would have asked simple questions: What are you going to do? What can you say about the likely outcome? When will we see individual behavior turn your spending into tax revenue? And I would have had no answers that would have stood up to the rigorous demands any treasury has on suggested spending programs.

So, if governments are not the place to go for insights into policy change to meet the new world, could the labor market itself be a source of hope? I would argue not. In most countries, an iron triangle of government, labor unions, and employer organizations has formed the strongest insider/outsider environment known to man. The labor market is not a market—it is a cartel for insiders.

Let me cite my native Sweden as an example. The labor market there consists of some 4.5 million people, and the turnover is extremely high; in a normal year, more than a million jobs change hands (which is different from saying that a million people change jobs). This shows that the labor market is very flexible—for those already employed. For those who lose their jobs, there is a plethora of support mechanisms: a nationwide public employment service to help them find new jobs, a generous unemployment insurance system, and so on. There are even agreements in place between trade unions and employers in which a sum is set aside each year for "transitional funds" to provide those being terminated with training and matching for new jobs during the termination period. And on-the-job training to keep employees competences up to date is common both in larger and smaller companies.

For the outsiders, the situation is much worse. Those who have never entered or who have lost their place in the labor market have a very hard time entering and reentering it. The young, the long-term unemployed, the immigrants and refugees (of whom we have a lot in Sweden) all face a very dire situation. Statistics show that the youth unemployment rate is four times higher than the regular unemployment rate, and that the unemployment rate for those born outside Sweden is some three times higher than it is for natives. On average, it takes newly arrived immigrant adults between seven and eleven years to get a permanent job. It is a disgrace.

Why is this? I would argue that it is a structural problem. Sweden has a long history of strong trade unions and employer organizations that take responsibility for relations in the labor market, including the wage formation process. Even for me as an old center-right politician, this has led to positive results. Over time, the Scandinavian model has created an environment of predictability for production, peace in the workplace, very few days lost to strikes, and a wage formation model that has been overall quite responsible and sound. To lean on Churchill once more, the model might be the worst one we know, except for all the others that have been tried.

For governments of all colors, this model has been comfortable. The wage formation process occurs with no political involvement. Trade unions are responsible, for the most part, and the relationship between employers and employees is mostly respectful and peaceful.

Of course, the clear downside to this is that those outside are very much excluded. The young, the immigrants, and the long-term unemployed have no unions, no congresses, no ombudsmen, no lobby groups, and no power. They are left outside this extremely strong iron triangle of government, unions, and employers. In what ways are they left outside? The clearest example is the way entry-level pay has been pushed up over the years, which effectively excludes those with no experience or low productivity from the labor market. Another example is the way public programs and social security work; the spending per average on insiders by far outweighs spending on the outsiders. In some perverse cases, public programs even discouraged outsiders from trying to get in. Until 2007, for example, those on disability pension were forbidden from even registering as jobseekers at the Public Employment Service and would risk their entire pension if they tried a job and failed.

In most cases, outsiders are seen as problems to be handled, when in effect they are promises to be delivered. Demographics show that the Swedish labor market is some 300 000 people short if we want to keep up our standard of living, and our public spending, in the decades to come. Simply put: we need more taxpayers and the only way we will achieve that is to turn outsiders to insiders.

As a minister, I would sleep with the Beveridge Curve under my pillow. The Beveridge Curve shows the correlation between unemployment and vacancies, and is seen as the best evidence of the mismatch in the labor market in which the employers are asking for one thing and the unemployed have something else to offer. Almost all modern unemployment policies have tools trying to rectify this mismatch, such as training programs, active labor market programs, vocational training, on-the-job training, reskilling, upskilling, and so on.

What I have come to believe is that there is something fundamentally wrong with the way we attack this problem. Today's understanding of the labor market is based on an individual jobseeker's offering 100 percent of his or her time to one employer and thus becoming full-time employed. He or she gets "a job." But what if all that is changing?

I believe we are moving from the traditional conception of "a job" to something similar to a "portfolio theory of work." Having "a job" will be less and less common. Instead, the demands of employers and companies will not be for unemployed workers but for those offering a mix of competences. These competences will not come 100 percent molded into one individual.

Similarly, more and more people are not willing to be employed in the old way. The freedom of matching projects into a portfolio of work is more attractive, especially to younger people, than the idea of working for twenty-five years at the same monotonous job just for the pleasure of getting a gold watch at the end of their careers.

Just visit an accelerator or incubator and you will see what I mean. At these creative places, swarms of people get together in loosely defined project teams for shorter or longer periods, trying to solve different problems and tasks. Is it so hard to see that other parts of the economy are in need of similar ways of re-organizing themselves to better reach and attract both talent and creativity?

To my mind, the long-term answer to the problem of the Beveridge Curve moving in the wrong direction lies not in retraining individuals for full-time employment, but rather in developing all of their skills and competences so they can offer them not as bundles but as sets. As the trends move toward the "de-bundling" of the individual unemployed, their return to work would be made possible by their offering sets of competences to a number of constituents or principals. These would be the core elements of a portfolio theory of work.

The fast pace of the economy is developing; changing and disappearing value chains and ever-increasing automation and digitalization will add speed and intensity to this development. Jobs are already disappearing, but I believe that there is still plenty of work out there that needs to be done. We just have to organize it differently.

Of course, there also are very strong forces out there trying to stop or slow down these changes. The insiders will want to keep things as they are. The members of the iron triangle will fight hard to preserve their relative power within the existing systems. Unions will fight for their power in the bargaining processes and want to define the labor market so that it fits them. Companies will resist change and want to preserve short-term profits. And governments will keep trying to solve twenty-first-century problems with twentieth-century policy tools.

But there is hope: nothing can stand in the way of a revolution whose time has come. And it is time for the labor market to develop from a cartel for the insiders to a market for the de-bundled unemployed to find work rather than "a job." And I am sure this will happen sooner or later anyway. To quote the Borg in *Star Trek*: "Resistance is futile."

There are, however, significant problems and issues to be dealt with in this new situation. The most important is the individual's need for economic security in the short term, as well as throughout life. Without that sense of security, many people will resist these changes at first and will continue to believe that they are subject to unacceptable risks when the changes do take place.

People who mix projects rather than having a single job will have a very difficult time getting a mortgage under today's rules and regulations. What do they do about pensions? Medical plans? Social security? How do they even out the flow of work so as to have an even distribution of work over the year? What about taxes? Vacation? And what will the wage formation process look like?

There is a risk that people will be empowered in principle but left to fend for themselves in a more brutal world, fighting for piecemeal projects, running between employers, principals, and customers—or simply being left behind.

Who the winners will be is obvious: the entrepreneurial go-getters who are competent and specialized, and can fend for themselves and market themselves. If everyone else will be at risk of becoming a loser, it is to be expected that politicians and governments will try to curtail this development. Allowing people to fend for themselves not only would seem unfair, but also would be bad politics. Losers are voters, too.

I would argue that those who are less entrepreneurial need not be losers in the future— on the contrary. Again, demographics show an increasing need for work to be done, and so the power rests in the hands of those offering to work. And if governments would spend more time assisting in the development of economic security systems that help and support the mixing of work and not just employment as we know it, the individual risk to the less entrepreneurial would diminish.

Companies, I am sure, also will develop tools for these new possibilities, offering more and more people a way to mix work rather than just setting them up with a job. Moreover, the old job agencies will have to transform into more Uber-like enterprises. Tomorrow, not only the will cabdrivers find work through an app, but so will other people.

To my mind, this is the time in history when we have a chance to move from the old Tayloristic and cartel-like labor market model to a model based on the real empowerment of individuals. This model would make it possible for people to mix and match, to plan their working lives in the short run and over the life cycle to adapt to their personal needs rather than to the needs of a single employer. For example, I could choose to work a bit less when my children are young and more when I am more experienced. I could choose to work with many projects and principals so that I find the colleagues and projects where my talent, skills, and personality are better recognized, rather than being stuck in a situation where I feel unappreciated and trapped for life.

Governments can play a crucial part in assisting in this development by recognizing that it is happening and then looking into its long-term consequences and determining how to mitigate the risks and downsides and assist those who have the most to gain from moving from "a job" to "work." Who are they, then? To my mind, those in position to gain the most from the power of the portfolio theory of work are those trapped in the 9-5, corporate ladder, never-ending treadmill kind of working life. In addition, there are all those who are underemployed or totally excluded from the labor market today. Now, that is not a bad target group for voter-hungry politicians.

My advice to governments would be to prepare for the wave, analyze its probable outcomes, find solutions to the problems which might occur, break out of the iron triangles, and come out as the winner as their citizens become more empowered, their labor markets become better equipped to handle change, and their economies become stronger. And I would advise them that, frankly, the alternative is to doom themselves to a slow death—that this is happening anyway, so it is up to them to decide whether their country is a winner or a loser.

CHAPTER 7

Developing Middle Class Jobs in a Digital Economy

By Geoffrey Moore[1]

Digital innovation is reengineering our manufacturing-based, product-centric economy to improve quality, reduce costs, expand markets, increase profits, and reward investment—all of which are very good things. It is doing so, however, largely at the expense of traditional middle class jobs. This class of work is bifurcating into elite professions that are highly compensated but outside the skillset of the target population and commoditizing workloads for which the wages fall well below the target level. Some have called this the "hollowing-out" of the middle class.

It is not proper to call this outcome *unjust*, for it is the result of positive economic activity conducted under rule of law. Moreover, while it is deeply challenging to societies with developed economies, the offshoring dimension of this movement, something enabled by digital innovation, has proved hugely helpful to developing economies in building their own middle class, albeit atop a much lower commodity wage base. So there is good to be had here.

Nonetheless, it is proper to call these changes *destabilizing* and *threatening to national and international interests*. Liberal democracy's success has long been linked to a vibrant middle class united in a common aspiration to see their children enjoy a lifestyle equal

---

1   Geoffrey Moore is an author, speaker, and advisor whose life's work has focused on the market dynamics surrounding disruptive innovations.

to or better than their own. When such aspirations cease to be realistic, people are no longer willing to make the sacrifices that make civil society work, and conditions deteriorate rapidly. as we have seen in countless failed and failing states around the world.

There are strong incentives, therefore, for both the public and private sectors to intercede on behalf of middle class interests. This can consist of a portfolio of strategies, including protectionism, wealth redistribution, cost of living reduction, and job creation. Protectionism and wealth redistribution are tactics to ameliorate the short-term effects of drastic dislocations, but neither is sustainable as a long-term strategy. Sooner or later, efficient economic entities take their toll on protected ones, and wealth finds a way to slip out from under even the most stringent societal controls. Cost of living reduction, on the other hand, is a sustainable strategy, particularly when it is linked to new sources of income, even if those be modest. This is the engine driving the new collaborative economy springing up around digital enterprises such as eBay, Etsy, Uber, Airbnb, and the like.

That said, by far the most sustainable strategy for developed economies is to develop proactively net new middle class job creation at scale. The question is, how in the world do we do that?

The basic metaphor I propose we keep in mind here is sailing, the critical success factors being boat, wind, and course. In the context of middle class job creation, the sailboat itself is the new job, the wind is the economic value that pays for that job, and the course is the positioning of the new jobs to catch the prevailing winds.

So what are the new winds blowing that will fund the next generation of middle-class jobs? Basically, jobs come into being around opportunities to release trapped value in economic systems. If that value can be tapped and transformed into an economic offer, it creates the net new cash flows that fund net new jobs. And, if those jobs match up to our targeted criteria for middle-class job creation—complex enough to warrant a middle-class wage while replicable enough to scale across a sufficiently broad population—then we are well underway.

To understand how this theory of trapped value plays out, consider the following "trickle down" framework for the life cycle of an economic innovation:

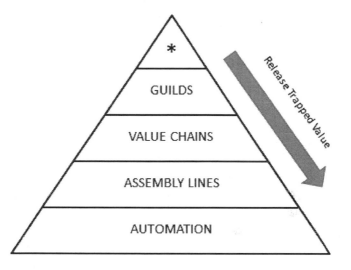

The asterisk in this diagram stands for entrepreneurs. These are the people who discover a new source of trapped value and invent a way to release it. Their inventions can create whole new sectors of the economy, as we have seen with automobiles, radio and television, telecommunications, computers, and the World Wide Web. At the outset, however, being confined to a single company, they have very little impact on overall job creation,

Job creation begins in earnest when an entrepreneurial success spawns an emerging ecosystem of companies to support and expand the new category. Much of the expertise required is still nascent, so the nature of this work is highly complex. Nonetheless, in order to scale, it must be made replicable to some degree. Enter the world of highly paid professionals, an elite class of deeply talented individuals who can capture and package lessons learned as they take on heretofore unsolved problems. In the Silicon Valley economy of today, think data scientists, user experience designers, cloud computing architects, and the like. For this class of work, the amount of trapped value released per person employed is spectacular, which is why these individuals can command extraordinary salaries and eye-popping signing bonuses.

Over time, as the number of these jobs expands to a point of equilibrium, as the disciplines of these professions become more stable and complete, and as educational systems catch on to and up to the opportunity, a guild model unfolds in which expertise is developed through apprenticeship, and quality is maintained through certification. At this stage, these are highly paid professions, not middle-class jobs in and of themselves, but they represent legitimate aspirations for the children of middle-class parents, representing as they do a very fast track to upward mobility. This is why people scrimp and save to send their children to college.

That said, it is the next transition, the one from guilds to value chains, that provides the fundamental engine of middle-class growth, the wind that will fill a flotilla of sails. At this point in the innovation life cycle, the guilds that helped capture the value at an earlier stage are now holding that value captive. Their overall workload has expanded beyond the complexity that warrants their expertise to an increasing number of low-value tasks that do not. Their economic model, however, persists in keeping the entire workload within their guild, thereby trapping value.

This can manifest itself in two very different forms, one represented by the manufacturing sector of the twentieth century, the other by the service sector of the twenty-first century. In a manufacturing context, companies leverage the "secret sauce" of their guild-maintained intellectual property to build end-to-end, vertically integrated enterprises, selling their goods and services at a premium by virtue of their differentiating core. This is what fueled the rise of General Motors and Ford, Merck and Pfizer, Xerox and IBM. At the outset, this actually works to everyone's advantage, for even though there is a mix of high- and low-value work, quality and accountability for end-to-end integration is maintained, and that in itself is worth the premium. But over time, as the innovation life cycle matures and the proportion of low- to high- value work increases, operating expenses balloon—creating trapped value. This was the wind that filled the sails of the business process reengineering movement of the 1980s and 1990s, led by the proliferation of client-server enterprise resource planning systems and widespread outsourcing, both of which drove enormous middle-class job growth at tier one and tier two suppliers in manufacturing, procurement, transportation, and logistics, not to mention information technology and professional services.

In the twenty-first century, much of that trapped value in the manufacturing sector has been released—hence the need to find new targets to support middle class job creation. For reasons we will dig into more deeply later on this essay, it is now the services sector that offers the best opportunities. In particular, a residual guild structure has created enormous amounts of trapped value in multiple social services, most notably in legal services, higher education, and health care. Costs in all three areas are out of proportion to value delivered, not because the service is bad but because it is overburdened with low-value workloads.

The trapped value referenced above comes from paying guild rates for work that does not warrant the guild wage premium. The solution to this problem is to evolve from the guild model to the value chain.

Value chains disaggregate guild workloads into clusters of tasks, each of varying complexity, and for each cluster, recruit companies best suited to perform its workload in a cost-effective way. Each cluster provides highly specialized expertise, and all are networked together to deliver the end-to-end benefit the market is paying for.

This network-of-specialists model outperforms the integrated generalist model, because each company's investments in human capital and capital equipment can be focused on their highest returning activities (the area of their specialization) while leaving the remaining workloads to other members of the value chain that specialize in that kind of work. To be fair, value chains can outperform guilds only wherever the network itself is efficient—meaning its transaction costs are low—hence the value of public sector investment in infrastructure and rule of law necessary for these networks to perform efficiently.

The reason value chains are terrific engines of middle-class employment is that each segment of the chain creates its own "mini-guild." These centers of expertise are one level of complexity reduced from the overarching guild capability, so the work is scalable to a much larger population. At the same time, it is still sufficiently complex to warrant a wage that supports a middle-class lifestyle.

So we will definitely be digging deeper into the transition from guild to value chain to develop winning strategies for middle-class job creation. But before we do, we need to complete the arc of the innovation lifecycle to incorporate lower layers which attack the trapped value now to be found inside middle-class jobs themselves. Again, we might wish to protect the middle class against the incursions of these lower layers, but by so doing we would be swimming against the tide of increased productivity— conceivably an appropriate tactic, but never a good strategy.

As value chains mature and segment, overall complexity eventually becomes sufficiently disaggregated that some workloads can be reengineered as sequences of commoditized tasks. This represents the transition from value chains to assembly lines. It dramatically expands the number of workers one can employ but at the cost of reducing wages well below the level required to support a middle-class lifestyle. Thus, process industrialization—the point at which outsourcing, the key to value chains, meets offshoring, the key to wage reduction through wage arbitrage—becomes the bane of middle-class employment in developed economies even as it becomes the source of such employment in developing economies. The best thing the developed economy and the middle class can say about this change of affairs is that it helps to reduce their consumer cost of living.

Finally, managing large populations of lower-wage workers has its own issues with trapped value, as enterprises find it increasingly problematic to maintain quality, to lower cost, and to address the social pressures engendered, all at the same time. Enter automation, the goal being to transfer truly commoditized high-volume workloads to a wage-free computerized system. This has the same dislocating effect on entry-level employment that offshoring has on middle class employment, although it is more often manifested by a stubbornly low minimum wage—essentially exploiting the entry-level workers' lack of bargaining power—than by the elimination of entry-level jobs altogether. Public policy can and often should intercede on behalf of the entry-level class, most obviously by legislating a minimum wage, but once again, swimming against the tide of productivity improvement is not a sustainable strategy. Where automation can do the work, normally automation should do the work, and human ingenuity should be applied to finding new sources of entry-level work.

Thus unfolds the trickle-down theory of job generation through successive reengineering of incumbent processes to release trapped value. With this overall framework in mind, let us now direct our attention to the middle band in the pyramid, the place where workloads are complex enough to warrant middle class wages yet sufficiently well characterized to be mastered by middle-class expertise. There are three paths into this zone, and they correspond to policy investments that create a return in the short, middle, and long run as follows:

Three Paths to Middle Class Job Creation

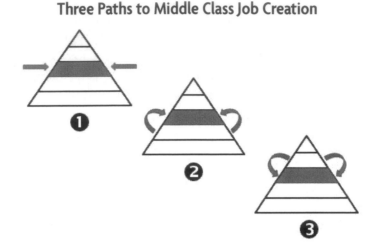

1. **Short-term, modest relief.** Start a new small business, right in the middle of the value chain zone, supplementing an existing value chain with a more targeted, differentiated, niche-focused offering, leveraging ubiquitous low-cost digital infrastructure to do so.

2. **Medium-term, significant relief.** Train members of the entry-level workforce in the band below to qualify for higher-value jobs in the band above them, focusing specifically on services functions that require empathy and cannot therefore be readily commoditized, including sales, customer service, marketing, technical support, human resources, and financial administration.

3. **Long-term, dramatic relief.** Invest in the value chain model itself to reengineer high-cost sectors of the service economy where the guild model has trapped value and bloated expenses, focusing on legal services, higher education, and health care, thereby both lowering the cost of living and growing middle class employment.

Let's look at each of these three paths in turn.

Path #1—Start a New Business in the Middle of an Existing Value Chain

The type of business we are talking about here is one that targets a niche market that is too small for the existing value chain to serve profitably. It does so with specialized offerings which are communicated directly to the target customers. Such businesses differentiate by virtue of their highly focused commitment to go the extra mile for a class of customer willing to pay a premium for such service. Historically, these businesses were not economical to create, because there were not enough local customers to get to a sustainable scale, and because the costs of marketing, sales, procurement, manufacturing, logistics, and finance created too great an overhead burden. None of these restrictions are the case today.

First of all, the World Wide Web allows a small business to access prospective customers around the world—for free! With a billion or so Web users to select from, even the smallest niche can be big enough to matter. Second, the Web also represents a network of service providers who are more than willing to outsource any function small business owners believe is either non-differentiating (hence a waste of their time) or outside the scope of their expertise (and hence a potential showstopper)—and to do so at highly competitive rates. And third, seed funding for starting these businesses is now also accessible over the Web via crowdsourcing mechanisms that let people invest in people they believe in—not just in business plans from proven executives with strong credit ratings.

That said, the challenge here is to knit all these resources together behind a business offer that is truly differentiated and actually does resonate with the target market. This requires coaching and support, very much along the lines of services provided by business incubators, but absent all the emphasis on technology per se. The offer itself can be very low-tech indeed—it is the coordination to bring everything together that has to be sophisticated. Incubators can attract talent to teach these skills and, just as important, to foster peer-to-peer relationships to share lessons learned and provide moral support.

Truly small business gestation is a great way to kick-start middle-class job creation, but it is limited in its ability to scale. Indeed, it really is not about job creation at all. The business owners themselves are the middle-class income earners, self-employed. The jobs they have created are their own, and it may be a long while before their businesses require a second employee, and even longer before that second job warrants a middle-class wage. For these reasons, we need to turn our attention to the second of our three paths forward.

Path #2—Train Members of the Entry-Level Workforce for Higher-Paid Jobs

The second path focuses on the currently scaled economy where, as we have seen, middle-class manufacturing jobs have been decimated by offshoring to lower-wage economies. One of the consequences of this shift, however, is that manufacturing as a function is no longer a source of product differentiation. Indeed, the entire product-centric model for an industrial economy is being reconfigured around a "services-first" model, in which businesses and consumers alike are subscribing to a set of outcomes as opposed to purchasing an item of inventory. Thus, General Electric Aircraft Engines is now offering its airline customers the option to buy "flight power" as a service, sold by the number of miles flown, with GE taking care of all the product and service logistics needed to deliver that outcome. Can GE Medical be far behind? And how about Amazon's Web Services, which sells "elastic computing" upon demand? Meanwhile, on the consumer side, digital services are sweeping the nation, finding their way into our lives through smartphones and tablets, paid for by transaction fees or by advertisers seeking an audience for their messaging.

In a services-led economy, the spotlight now falls on the services-oriented functions, particularly the ones that are customer-facing. In addition to our service delivery systems work, inevitably there are issues to negotiate before, during, and after the sale, and negotiation is an irreducibly complex activity that requires understanding, judgment, and empathy beyond the scope of an entry level worker. At the same time, these issues are sufficiently recurrent that enterprises can build playbooks and policies to keep their complexity within bounds. In short, we have here the core requirements for supporting a middle class wage.

The intervention required here is training, but not of the sort generally conceived in job training programs. The goal is not to master a body of technical material; the goal is to develop a body of interpersonal skills. It is not about knowledge or even experience; it is about aptitude and attitude. Enterprises are more than willing to train a new employee on the specifics of their business, so when they are hiring, especially for market-facing services functions, they are looking for interpersonal skills in someone who looks to be a good fit for their culture.

In this context, one of the most accessible opportunities for the foreseeable future will be online sales and customer support, delivered over the Web, leveraging email, chat, audio, and video interactions. Unlike sales jobs of the past, which focused on hard-nosed closing tactics, this new medium rewards listening, responding, and collaborating in ways that are equally satisfying to customer and employee alike. This opens the aperture to a much broader pool of candidates, many of whom have hung back in the past, because they have heard too many bad things about "being in sales." Public policy can make a significant contribution here by working with the private sector to develop a new "customer-facing skills" curriculum, one that is better suited to our new digital world.

This second path represents a middle-term solution, because developing this training and provisioning it at scale will take some lead time. And it has the potential for significant, but not dramatic, impact on middle class employment, because the trapped value comes from second-order effects of an otherwise reasonably well functioning system. At the end of the day, the really big impact occurs when trapped value is so great as to actually be pricing the offer out of its target customer's reach, and for that we need to turn to our third zone of opportunity.

Path #3—Invest in the Value Chain Model Itself to Reengineer High-Cost Sectors of the Service Economy

The third opportunity is to focus on releasing the trapped value in those parts of the service sector where the guild model has long overstayed its welcome. In the context of the U.S. economy, this applies in particular to legal services, higher education, and health care. All three comprise a broad range of workloads, from the irreducibly complex to the routine and mundane, the bulk of which are still being delivered by a certified set of highly paid professionals. Much of their workload can and should be offloaded to a paraprofessional supporting class of workers, but today it must by law or custom be done by these same highly paid workers. This is not only economically inefficient but also diverts them from more value-adding work, and is deeply tiring to boot. Not surprisingly, morale in all three professions is suffering even as costs to deliver their services continue to escalate. It is past time to intervene.

The primary challenge here is structural, not personal. Each profession still operates as a guild. In the United States, it is illegal to deliver legal services unless you are a member of a law firm. In higher education, well-paid faculty positions go only to tenured professors, and in medicine, all but the most routine tasks are restricted to certified doctors. Membership in these guilds provides structural control over the economics of that profession, including the power to block access from competing sources of service. Legislation reinforces this blocking power, as does tradition, the net effect being that all three sectors are well and truly stuck. Worst of all, none has an economic incentive to move, so even though many would move forward as individuals, the institutions themselves are entrenched.

The consequence of these dynamics is that all three services are pricing themselves out of the market. Corporations are no longer willing to underwrite high legal fees for relatively routine legal work. Students and their parents are no longer willing to take on consuming debt to get a college diploma. And health care insurers are no longer willing to underwrite inefficient medical practices because the doctor knows best. The winds of change are blowing, and the very best thing leaders in these three sectors could do is to use the value chain transformation to get out ahead of this problem.

To do so, they are going to need the active support of both the public and private sectors. On the public side, there are regulatory regimes, particularly in health care and legal services, that need to be revamped. On the private side, all three institutions need room to experiment with new business models that do not conform to the letter of existing contract commitments. And all three could do with a large dose of the "design thinking" that is helping other sectors of the economy work through their transformations.

In the context of such value chain reengineering, what kind of workloads are we talking about? Our first criterion is that they be sufficiently complex to warrant a middle-class wage while sufficiently constrained to yield to a playbook approach. In addition, we want to target large workloads that are budget busters, areas where systemic productivity improvement would not only create middle-class jobs but also dramatically lower overall costs. Examples include negotiating customer contracts and handling consumer dispute resolution in legal services, teaching required courses in freshman writing and introductory seminars for university freshmen and sophomores, and managing first-level health care issues in family medicine and eldercare practices. But these are just the tip of the iceberg. If the lessons of reengineering the manufacturing sector have taught us anything, it is that the opportunities are legion, and the value chain model is well equipped both to discover and to remediate them.

That said, this third path is a longer-term strategy than either of the prior two. Reengineering is always met with suspicion and resistance, and it takes time for a supportive social contract to emerge. But once it does, the savings gained pay for continual expansion, funding wave after wave of next-generation jobs. This is the economic engine we need to get turning now.

Final Remarks

In closing, let me surface one final concern that is inherent in the trapped value model of innovation. Every time one reengineers a process to release trapped value, someone's ox gets gored. For the guild, it is gored by the middle class; for the middle class, by the entry-level worker; and for the entry-level worker, by automation. And then there is a larger existential question: Won't we eventually run out of oxen to gore? And if that is the case, why would we want to adopt policies that accelerate to this end? Aren't we simply acting out the myth of Sisyphus?

No, actually we are acting out the narrative of Darwinism. All economies are competitions for scarce resources, and all these competitions have losers as well as winners. But they do not have to be zero-sum games. The guild continues to create enormous value but does so within the bounds of a complexity that warrants its premium. The same goes for the middle and entry-level classes. It is just that the work itself is continually maturing, and thus the work must continually reach out and embrace newer workloads as older ones commoditize.

Moreover, there is an inherently progressive element in the history of this process. At the end of any arc of innovation, when we have gone all the way from entrepreneur to automation, goods and services that used to be scarce and very expensive to acquire now have been made plentiful and cheap. That makes them a perfect platform upon which to build the next wave of innovation. Entrepreneurs are the ones who catch on to the implications of this new state the fastest. They kick off the next round of innovation, they launch the next arc. There may indeed be no rest for the weary, but there also is no end to this parade.

In this context, the role of public policy and private investment is to help the economy expand by working its way down through the stages of this framework, while at the same time helping the workforce to increase its wages by finding next-generation workloads that still require the skills that warrant their premium. Holding on to the old workloads, propping up wages no longer warranted by the value delivered—these may be used tactically in times of great disruption, but they cannot be the basis for any lasting social programs.

CHAPTER 8

The Supercritical Human Elevated [SHE] Economy

By Monique Morrow[1]

Abstract

With another three billion people coming online in the next six years, companies are racing to capture the emerging market. Their efforts include developing new, innovative ways of blanketing the whole planet with Internet service. Smartphones, tablets and computers are dropping in price, flowing into the low-cost markets. At this time, the cheapest smartphone costs only twenty dollars.

As this market emerges, the SHE Platform for a Supercritical Human Elevated Economy will reach women everywhere with the education, skills, collaboration, and jobs to lift them out of poverty and to create "SHEntrepreneurs."

SHE Hands Women the Ropes in the Innovation Economy

Women will be able to use the open SHE platform to deliver services that citizens will consume. The vision is to create an Internet of women job creators for the global economy.

1   Monique Morrow is the Chief Technology Officer–Evangelist for New Frontiers Development and Engineering at Cisco.

Women will build on GitHub, the largest host and community for open source code in the world, which today hosts more than nine million users and more than twenty-one million repositories. SHE is consistent with GitHub's slogan, "Build software better, together." SHEntrepreneurs will use the SHE platform to build foundational code skills and to connect to other women entrepreneurs all over the world—it is a resource discovery system.

What about the "Missing" Element for Achieving SHE?

These efforts to foster innovation, creativity, and a firsthand approach to achieving growth of course require fresh minds—generations and people who are willing to grab the bull by its horns, perhaps not to tame it but to lead it. In this case, the bull is technology, and the riders are those who are willing to make the best use of this machinery.

For many reasons, creating a bull-leaders category would be hard to accomplish without getting everyone involved. Everyone here is precisely linked to the "missing" in our society: women. The discussion about innovation for jobs definitely needs to be correlated to advancing gender security and to empowering women economically through their own efforts, ultimately creating a greater sense of value within them and encouraging them to unleash the groundbreaker within.

Women as the "Missing" Sex

For many years, as a result of complicated social structures around the world, women have been excluded from the show. This can vary from culture to culture, town to city, rural to urban community, and so on. As shocking as this might sound—or maybe it is to be expected—the facts have not changed that much since the World Bank published its report on "missing women" in 2012.[2]

2 World Bank. *World Development Report 2012: Gender Equality and Development*. 2012, https://openknowledge.worldbank.org/handle/10986/4391.

The report found that women represent 40 percent of the world's labor force but hold just 1 percent of the world's wealth. For every one dollar that men earn, salaried women workers earn sixty-two cents in Germany, sixty-four cents in India, and about eighty cents in Mexico and Egypt. Women entrepreneurs fare far worse, earning thirty-four cents in Ethiopia and just twelve cents in Bangladesh for every dollar that men earn.

These numbers reflect the inequality in income for women and ultimately indicate that women are not being appreciated. When a woman is fully dedicated to her work but gets much less recognition from the other sex, it can hinder her productivity and disrupt the progress of her business. She will feel unjustly treated and may experience other negative emotions that cause her to shy away from what she is doing.

The World Bank emphasizes this idea in its 2012 report and concludes that "countries that create better opportunities and conditions for women and girls can raise productivity, improve outcomes for children, make institutions more representative, and advance development prospects for all."[3]

Another factor that impedes the role of women as effective decision-makers in society is mortality. According to the World Bank's 2012 report, women and girls are more likely to die, relative to men and boys, in low- and middle-income countries than are their counterparts in wealthier countries, with 3.9 million "missing" women and girls each year under the age of sixty. At least 40 percent of those are never born, one-sixth die in infancy, and one-third die in their reproductive years. The problem is worst in Sub-Saharan Africa and countries hit by HIV/AIDS.[4]

---

3 World Bank. "Gender Equality: The Right and Smart Thing to Do – World Bank Report," Press Release No.:2012/065/DEC, September 18, 2011, http://web.worldbank.org/WBSITE/EXTERNAL/NEWS/0,,contentMDK:23003001~pagePK:6425 7043~piPK:437376~theSitePK:4607,00.html.
4 World Development Report 2012: Gender Equality and Development. Pg. xxi.

Ethnic Barriers

The problem in education is a bit different; it is not about being "missing" but about being of a certain ethnicity. Women now account for more than half of the world's university students, and sixty countries have more young women than men in universities. In primary education, disparities between boys and girls have closed in almost all nations. And in secondary education, girls now outnumber boys in forty-five developing countries. But ethnicity combined with poverty can be a barrier: two-thirds of out-of-school girls around the world belong to ethnic minority groups.

What is the problem when it comes to education, then? Well, unfortunately the answer to this question is patriarchy. There are cultural barriers—namely, values that are patriarchal—that obviate these opportunities. These values are rooted in roles relating to marriage, family, and work that traditionally have been attributed to men and women and have evolved over the past several centuries.

A woman can be well educated, intelligent, and skilled, but still be not allowed to opt for certain jobs. In some communities, she will have an "authority" (a brother, father, husband, jealous boyfriend) telling her she cannot attend a certain conference or be present in a community where males prevail.

This has been particularly apparent in the recent protests in the Middle East, particularly Lebanon. Men from across the region were making comments about the physical appearance of women, totally disregarding the fact that they all were there to call for social change. If men cannot take women seriously when they take to the streets to demand change, how are they supposed to take them seriously at work?

With a set of norms that makes men think they are the heads of everything, men will definitely feel reluctant to have females as their bosses. One Arab woman told me that she believes that it may take at least two or three generations to change the value system.

"We attend university, as ingrained in our culture, not for a job or profession, and even if we have progressive husbands, we are still expected to be home and perform the household duties expected of a wife and mother," she said. "The father is absent from child rearing, other than being a financial source."

So, yes, the natural inclination is to hope and aspire to be a contributing member of society. For men in societies with such values, this is easy and effortless, but for women, it is a continuing struggle.

The brutal gang rape and murder of Jyoti Singh Pandey in New Delhi in December 2012 confirmed the challenges women—and men—have to move out of a subjugating caste system. The young woman aspired to be a schoolteacher, and her father sold his land and worked double shifts to pay for her schooling.

In an interview, he related that, as a youth, he had dreamed of becoming a schoolteacher, but at that time education was not considered important, and girls were not even sent to school. "Attitudes are changing back home now, but when I left thirty years ago, I vowed to never deny my children, so sending them to school was fulfilling my desire for knowledge," he said. He added that he put his daughter's education above that of even his two sons. "It never entered our hearts to ever discriminate. How could I be happy if my son is happy and my daughter isn't? And it was impossible to refuse a little girl who loved going to school."

Apart from the support, or lack of support, that some families provide to their sons and daughters, there has been a serious new threat to the future of women in some regions. Time does seem to go backward instead of moving forward. There are many examples, such as the kidnapping in April 2014 of 276 female students from a government secondary school in Nigeria.

Girls in Nigeria now fear that, by seeking an education, they risk being kidnapped by the West African terrorist group Boko Haram, which would subject them to systematic rape. The terrorist group ISIL, on the other hand, is targeting Yazidi women as sex slaves, and, in an even more sinister development, is recruiting women to serve in its self-declared caliphate.

These threats not only affect the social and psychological aspects of a woman's life but also jeopardize her future. Some women, even if they do succeed in escaping from rape and slavery, may need decades to recover from the trauma they experienced and to be ready to enter the workforce again. They surely will remain missing for some while.

Gender Security and Youth

It is not only women who have been missing. Young people also have been excluded from opportunities to make change possible.

Globalization has made our world significantly smaller over the last few decades, but the size and range of our problems have barely changed. Despite all of our efforts to affect the status quo through the United Nations' Millennium Development Goals, which include promoting gender equality and empowering women, the same complex structural issues persist and affect billions worldwide. These are the results of our institutions.

But young people, aged fifteen to twenty-four, have been hard at work identifying and developing solutions to global problems, and this trend is not to be underestimated. The creative strategies that young people are using to tackle various elements of these widespread problems, from access to education and infrastructure development to sexual harassment and gender equality, have demonstrated the need to leverage technology in ways we had never imagined. Young people have spurred a newfound literacy in our approach to economic development and cooperative problem solving. Therefore, the priority must be to support driven young people who are striving to improve their communities.

Government and industry support is vital to achieving these goals at scale. We have seen disparate examples of such public-private partnerships steadily emerging around the world. Yet, while there is much conversation about supporting young people, there is a lack of action. Still, an international focus that prioritizes capturing and applying lessons from narratives of young people's innovation will engender limitless possibilities for sustainable transformation.

Today, the world's population numbers 7.3 billion and counting, with massive growth in the age twelve to twenty-four category. This demographic category is maturing in increasingly urbanized environments, where challenges of consumption are exacerbated by a lack of available or accessible resources. Instead of helping these young people raise their voices and involving them in the development of solutions, we often vilify them and exclude them from making policy or from contributing to real solutions.

Youth, government, and industry must work to surpass all previous landmarks of progress, and, in so doing, create an entirely new cooperative process of problem-solving in uncharted territory. The opportunities are nearly limitless when we connect the right talent, resources, and support, and so we must focus on supporting girls and promoting gender equality, on bringing the Internet to everyone, and on utilizing the low cost and accessibility of wireless technology to disseminate information and practical education.

As Marian Wright Edelman once stated, "If you don't like the way the world is, you change it. You have an obligation to change it. You just do it one step at a time." Working together, we will not only resolve the challenges we face but also make the impact of our combined efforts exponentially greater.

We have borrowed the earth from our children. It is past time that we empower them to redefine their reality and to create a world that surpasses what we have dreamt for them and goes far beyond past the boundaries of our imaginations and far into the future.

Aspiring to a SHE economy that integrates human values is an opportunity to innovate for jobs. This will mean more flow of ideas, more flow of innovation, and much more possibility for expansion.

For women, technology is the bull to be led. What is needed is to train more women to take the bull by its horns and to create a new generation of tech-females. Imagine disrupting unemployment via a global SHE economy platform powered by women using open source software and consumed via a smart device. Imagine disrupting the cultural barriers via the SHE platform.

The Technology of the SHE Platform

The open source will be a key modality for the SHE platform, while a block chain technology can retain a trust ledger for the platform. SHE application programming interface (API) governance will be via an auction mechanism to determine the value of a proposed API.

Open source is one of the more successful models that catalyzes innovation and leads to opportunities. It is available to anyone in the world and utilizes the power of the crowd to develop, modify, share, and improve. Mozilla Firefox and the Arduino board for robotics are examples of open-source software platforms that are used and improved by people around the world for free.

GitHub will provide the foundation for the SHE platform, enabling open-source collaboration and development. Women from all over the world can work together, learn from one another, and empower one another to succeed, all via access to the Internet and through smartphones and tablets.

Many startup companies are working on disrupting education in general, propelled by increased access to education through the Internet. Companies like XPRIZE are helping to catalyze innovation in the education space through multi-million dollar incentivized prizes to software developers who successfully develop self-instruction software that a child can learn to use with no human intervention. Imagine dropping a charged tablet into a remote village that had never seen a smartphone or tablet, and within hours the children would have not only figured out how to turn it on but also would have taught themselves to open and play with the applications.

To financially democratize the platform, block chain technology, also known as digital currency, can be employed. This technology uses multiple encryption techniques to regulate, record, and verify money transfers between parties, and operates completely independently of a traditional bank, without concern for geographical, cultural, religious, or political borders.

Rollout Strategy

The first stage in the rollout of the global SHE platform would be to launch a freemium model to encourage the use of the platform. The longer-term goal would be to develop a global public private partnership in which governments give tax breaks to enterprises—e.g., women for the world—that develop the SHE Platform, thereby stimulating its growth.

Can we not imagine developing the SHE platform to create a world in which gainful employment is divided fifty-fifty among men and women? Can we not imagine restoring the missing element in order to double productivity? We can if we dare!

CHAPTER 9

Innovation for Jobs with Cognitive Assistants: A Service Science Perspective

---

By Jim Spohrer[1]

Abstract

In the age of smart machines, rather than trying to predict the future of jobs, might it possible to assist each individual in the design of an optimal job? After all, untapped and unrealized human potential is perhaps the greatest waste of all time. Nordfors (2014) states: "If we become as innovative in creating good jobs as we are in creating innovative products and services, then the innovation economy is sustainable." This chapter explores the topic of innovation for jobs from a service science perspective, and suggests a path forward based on cognitive assistants for all occupations in smart, people-centered service systems.

Introduction: Motivation and Goals

Interactions among individual genes, or cells, or animals, among interest groups, or nations, or corporations, can be viewed through the lenses of game theory. What follows is a survey of human history, and of organic history, with those lenses in place. My hope is to illuminate a kind of force—the non-zero-sum dynamic—that has crucially

---

1 Jim Spohrer is Director of Global University Programs and Cognitive Systems Institute, IBM.

shaped the unfolding of life on earth so far.... In short, both organic and human history involve the playing of ever-more-numerous, ever-larger, and ever-more-elaborate non-zero-sum games. It is the accumulation of these games—game upon game upon game—that constitutes the growth of biological and social complexity.... (Wright 2000, 5–7)

—Robert Wright,
American author, journalist and scholar

Throughout most of human history, there were no jobs for money, just the daily toil of finding food and shelter to survive by working the local environment. Over the last ten millennia, with the growth of agriculture and cities, followed in the last few centuries by the growth of industrialization and further growth of cities, first extended families and then complexes of factories established ways of working for money, which could in turn be exchanged for that which could not be gathered, bartered, or made by family members. With rising wealth and technologies in the last dozen decades of human history, most national economies have witnessed the migration of jobs for money from agriculture and manufacturing to the so-called service sector. The service sector includes human services, such as government, health care, and education; business services, such as finance, information, and construction; consumer or experience services, such as retail, hospitality, and entertainment; and basic services, such as utilities, communication, transportation, and housing. While no sharp divisions can be imposed, the market for jobs for money has largely been provided by businesses and governments, which are organizations that require tasks be performed efficiently as a fiduciary duty. This fiduciary responsibility to act only in the interest of another entity, be it citizen taxpayers for governments or shareholder investors for businesses, is an important factor that drives these types of organizations to greater and greater levels of productivity.

Thus, a dilemma: the businesses and governments which gave rise to the market for jobs for money in the first place are now destroying jobs for money, as a result of their responsibility to stakeholders to perform efficiently and at the highest levels of quality in a task economy. For example, Foxconn has created hundreds of thousands, if not millions, of jobs in China, and is now aggressively embracing robotics, hitting a few speed bumps, but making steady progress eliminating the jobs for money they created in the last decade (Kan 2015). The task economy of businesses and governments is duty bound to demand more and more from higher-skilled workers/innovators, while at the same time seeking to replace routine workers/human capital with advanced technologies. For job creation innovators, one must ask, what higher-value, high-skill, people-intensive service offerings can these organizations provide their customers, while making the provision of routine offerings more efficient and thereby eliminating jobs? There is no law that says an innovation must create more jobs than it destroys. Make no mistake, as a taxpayer, I want my government to perform all tasks with the utmost productivity and quality, as long as the innovation processes are sustainable and comply with laws; likewise, as a shareholder, I want my businesses to perform all tasks with the utmost productivity and quality, as long as the innovation processes are sustainable and comply with laws. Nevertheless, if the task economy jobs all disappear, society will not function properly under the current rules of the game, so, clearly, a dilemma of massive proportions is emerging.

To be clear, the origin of the dilemma is that people in the task economy specialize, in accordance with Adam Smith's observations regarding the wealth of nations a few centuries ago. Specialization is a characteristic of the task economy, and, like any process of task decomposition, it eventually leads to automation to achieve efficiency goals and other productivity-related key performance indicators. Specialization is ultimately what makes people act like machines, and hence makes their work obsolete. So is specialization the enemy? Has the logic of Adam Smith finally run its course? Is a new logic required? Some say yes, and posit the end of capitalism (Mason 2015). Is there a way out of this dilemma, in which the largest job creators of one era must also become the largest job destroyers of another era, if they are performing their duties well?

As alarm bells are being sounded on multiple fronts (Brynjolfsson and MacAfee 2014; Dobbs et al. 2012; Wadhwa 2015), some have begun calling for and self-organizing to disrupt unemployment, to innovate for jobs, and perhaps to create a new trillion-dollar industry in the process (Nordfors 2014; Carlson 2015). For example, Jobly, the hypothetical startup envisioned by Nordfors, designs ideal jobs in a people-centered economy based on a person's unique capabilities and interests. Jobly does not exist, but if it did, it would be the ultimate social worker with expert job design skills. If Jobly could be built, everyone might become self-sufficient, and perhaps even wealthy, as a sole proprietorship with no distinction between the person and the small business; with Jobly as a partner for life, everyone could perfect "Me Inc." Although Jobly may sound a bit like the ultimate social worker, the role of social worker as a job for money exists within the structure of last century organizations with a responsibility to improve productivity and quality through sustainable innovation that is in turn based on knowledge-based technological advances. Social workers exist within the task economy that is also the innovation economy, and, therefore. additional rethinking of constraints is required if a true solution to the paradox is to be found.

As we will come to see from a service science perspective, a measurable role conflict is emerging. Jobs for money, the fiduciary responsibilities of governments and businesses, and the self-interest of taxpayers and shareholders are all increasingly at odds—because of the power of technology. Perhaps there is light at the end of this tunnel, in the form of cognitive assistants for all occupations in smart, people-centered service systems. However, first, to see this resolution more clearly, service science and the notion of smart, people-centered service systems must be introduced. The logic of a technology perspective might seem to lead to super-powered entities that no longer need others (e.g., needs, wants, and aspirations satisfied within a closed system), whereas the logic of a service science perspective is that of an evolving ecology of entities where communication is required to accelerate learning.

Service Science

So if we can measure how the members of a society spend their time, we have the elements of a certain sort of account of how that society works. And if we can make these sorts of measurements repeatedly, at different stages in the history of society, then we will have the basis for a developmental account of social and economic change." (Gershuny 2000, 1).

—Jonathan Gershuny, British social scientist

Paying others to perform a service wherein they apply their knowledge for your benefit is fundamental to modern society. For the purposes of developing a science of service, *service* can be defined as the application of knowledge for mutual benefit (Spohrer, Kwan, Fisk 2014). By this definition, division of labor can be viewed as service, and even products can be seen as embedding the knowledge or service of others (Bastiat 1850/1979; Lusch and Vargo 2014). Similarly, technologies can be seen as embedding knowledge and discoveries, or service from prior generations of people (Arthur 2009). Some have even proposed that the heirs of Newton should receive small payments every time an airplane flies or a car slows using a braking mechanism that embodies the laws of motion Newton described (Galambos 1998).

Service science is the study of the evolving ecology of nested networked service system entities, and their capabilities, constraints, rights, and responsibilities, as they apply knowledge for mutual benefit (Spohrer and Maglio 2010; Spohrer, Kwan, and Fisk 2014). Like biology two hundred years ago, service science has set about counting and classifying entities; but in the case of service science, the entities of interest are those capable of knowledge-based, value co-creation interactions. Service system entities include individuals, families, universities, cities, nations, businesses, foundations, and nonprofits, to name just a few types. Service science focuses on these diverse socio-technical entities and their value co-creation and capability co-elevation processes, interactions, and outcomes. As we will come to see, sustainably improving the quality of life generation over generation ultimately requires the mastery of repeatedly rethinking constraints and rebuilding service systems from scratch. Rapidly rebuilding complex systems from scratch is a type of mechanism, which can be observed in biological systems (e.g., seeds) and has benefits in certain social systems (e.g., education, construction).

There are perhaps twenty billion formal service system entities in the world today, each governed in part by formal written laws. Every person, household, university, business, and government is a formal service system entity, but my dog, my smartphone, and my ideas are not. New types of formal service system entities are created periodically when laws change —e.g., laws governing same-sex households or new types of public benefit corporations. The rights and responsibilities of entities matter.

Service science seeks to measure the productivity, quality, compliance, and sustainable innovation aspects of service system entities, as part of the evolving ecology of nested, networked entities. Each of these four measures corresponds to a relationship aspect of service systems: productivity corresponds to provider; quality, to customer; compliance, to authority; and sustainable innovation, to competitor. To remain viable, service systems entities, which are dynamic configurations of people, technology, organizations, and shared information connected internally and externally by value propositions, must learn and transform. Exponential change is subtle. An average, well-educated adult can possess much better models of the world than any individual did 100 years ago. So the exponential growth in knowledge and ability to apply knowledge rapidly foreshadows what might be possible, if a true purpose for individual education is achieved. Our species has the potential to take the next step beyond reading, writing, and arithmetic, and to create a generation of individuals inspired to build it better.

Practically speaking, people can comfortably change only at a rate determined by a number of factors. Teasing apart those factors is not easy. For example, because individuals are constrained by finite lifespans, the individuals who fill roles in the larger service ecology change from generation to generation (Spohrer et al. 2010). Throughout most of human history, these roles were not jobs for money, but in the past dozen decades, the rules of the game have changed (Spohrer et al. 2012). Because of the constraints of finite learning rates and bounded rationality, the mathematical advantages of specialization and association have fueled economic progress and the co-evolution of the growth of jobs for pay in businesses, governments, and universities (Smith 1776/199; Ricardo 1819/1971; Spohrer et al. 2013).

Put simply, the growth of knowledge has paralleled the growth in population and only recently bumped into the challenge of the "knowledge burden" (Jones 2009). Knowledge (human discovery) is growing faster than education's ability to transfer it to the next generation. The American Dream and quality of life for the next generation is about to get worse rather than better, if individuals do not become smarter fast.

Arguably, because of the constraints of finite lifespan, finite learning rates, and bounded rationality, the co-evolution of entities in the service ecology is optimized for knowledge accumulation in phase with the time constant of one generation of new workers (about twenty years, given current institutions and human biological constraints). In a sense, this represents a culturally comfortable rate of change for people, families, universities, businesses, and governments competing in a knowledge-driven task economy, and was the dominant time constant providing the context in which these service systems evolved in the past 200 years.

An analysis by the McKinsey Global Institute of U.S. economic data over almost a century showed that while shorter time periods experienced volatility in growth and employment, nearly all ten-year periods experienced both growth in gross domestic product and growth in employment (Dobbs et al. 2012). The argument can be made that at this time scale the available skills in the workforce and job opportunities offered by businesses and governments are matched. When reskilling the workforce happens slowly, universities can and do play an important role.

The problem of old jobs disappearing faster than new jobs are being created can be seen as a problem of time constants being mismatched among service system entities. One time constant is related to how quickly a person can learn new valuable skills, and another is related to how quickly organizations create and change jobs roles. As long as the old jobs that were being destroyed were low-skill, low-pay jobs with decreasing demand, there was no problem. However, today, even high-skill, high-pay jobs for which demand is growing are targets for technological automation. The fear is that reskilling will not be an option for many people displaced by rapidly advancing technological capabilities. Combined with the imperative of businesses and governments operating in a task economy to improve productivity and quality on a quarterly or election cycle basis, the time constants of service system entities are increasingly mismatched.

Smart, People-Centered Service Systems

> The faster an industry evolves—that is, the faster its clockspeed—the more temporary a company's advantage. The key is to choose the right advantage—again and again." (Fine 1998)
>
> —Charles H. Fine, American managerial scholar

Cognitive assistants exist or are being developed for a growing number of occupations. Spohrer and Banavar (2015) present two dozen examples, from chefs to CEOs, and from day care workers to doctors. In general, the cognitive assistants are helping people both with knowledge-intensive expert thinking and with complex communication among entities learning more rapidly from each other and their experiments. Levy and Murnane (2012) identify these factors as key attributes of occupations evolving in the context of advanced information and communication technologies.

Even lawn care is becoming more knowledge-intensive, and information and communication technologies accelerate the ability of entities to learn from the experiences of others.

The Occupational Information Network (O*NET) is a website that provides a description of nearly a thousand occupations that drive the U.S. gross domestic product. The Cognitive Systems Institute Group (CSIG) is a community dedicated to open sharing of best practices for improving methodologies to rapidly develop and evolve cognitive assistants for all occupations and societal roles (CSIG 2015). The mission of CSIG is to augment and scale expertise in smart, people-centered service systems. Furthermore, the National Science Foundation is funding faculty to study smart, human-centered service systems with the goal of accelerating the translation of research into economic impact on the U.S. (NSF 2014).

In the context of smart, people-centered service systems, cognitive systems (or "our cognitive mediators," as they may become known) can potentially progress from tools to assistants to collaborators to coaches, and be perceived differently depending on the role they play in a service system. To be people-centered, this progression requires that cognitive systems acquire better and better models of their users and more expert cognitive and social capabilities. Eventually, cognitive assistants will exist for all types of occupations and societal roles in service systems—and this will be the dawn of the era of smart, people-centered service systems. The ownership of cognitive systems and the personal data on which they will operate as they build user models will become an active area of legislation in coming years, as companies that produce intelligent personal assistants seek to monetize fully the benefits they create for customers (HAT 2015).

Kline (1995) and others tried to measure exponential change in socio-technical systems. The measurement of exponentials associated with service system entities is an important future research question in service science. Exponential improvement can be measured relative to (1) a measure based on existing set of units (e.g., kilometers per hour), (2) a measure that reflects a novel combinations of units (e.g., bits per joule), or (3) a measure that includes a novel unit of measure (e.g., trust).

As service science matures and the measurement of relevant exponentials is better understood, it might be possible to articulate a kind of Moore's law of service system improvement. Such a win-win-win for individuals, businesses, and governments would likely require reframing the competition for collaborators in the service ecology as a better non-zero-sum game than exists today using the concept of jobs for pay.

Concluding Remarks: Taking Responsibility

Civilization advances by extending the number of important operations which we can perform without thinking of them.

—Alfred North Whitehead, English mathematician

To our children and our children's children, to whom we elders owe an explanation of the world that is understandable, realistic, forward-looking, and whole.

—Stephen Jay Kline, American engineer

In 1985, very few people knew about cellphones or even the Internet, on which the World Wide Web would soon begin to take shape. Ten years later, by 1995, people in the developed nations were just beginning to get comfortable using cellphones to communicate and the World Wide Web to access information online. By 2015, just one college-age generation or twenty years later, nearly 20 percent of the global population has access to smartphones, combining the two capabilities and creating a co-creation platform for millions of developers. By 2035, students and professionals may very well be symbiotic with their cognitive assistants. Our cognitive mediators, depending on the context, will seem like a tool, an assistant, a collaborator, or a coach. If Moore's law holds, our personal cognitive mediators in 2035 will have the power of one human brain, but by 2055, many thousands of brains. Will

Jobly help us put those thousands of brains to good use? The problem will not simply be, what should I do to earn a living, but, what purpose should I direct my cognitive mediator toward to inspire the next generation to build it better?

The best way to predict the future is to inspire the next generation to build it. By 2035, our personal cognitive assistants may know us so well that they can represent us in many of the routine interactions with other people's cognitive assistants. Surely, as the capabilities and models of those they assist grow, they will be providing an income stream for their owners.

A service science perspective suggests that the application of knowledge for mutual benefit is a responsibility that each generation of entities has both to each other and to future generations. However, the burden of knowledge is growing, and so each generation must learn to rebuild from scratch better than previous generations have, as well as to add new knowledge. To inspire the next generation to build it better, we can ask them, will your generation be the generation to realize safer, more efficient transportation with driverless cars, and will your generation create more cities like Singapore that recycle 99 percent of their water? Will your generation bring manufacturing local again via robotics and 3D printers, make energy abundant via the artificial leaf and geothermal systems, show the way to creating building structures in hours that are more energy efficient, safer, and can also be recycled on demand? Will your generation be the first to be symbiotic with cognitive mediators, to revolutionize retail and hospitality with social media predicting our needs and wants seamlessly, while crowdfunding more zero-to-a-billion startups in less time, transforming health care, education, and government service systems so that they improve the weakest links in society, and not simply rewarding the strongest?

By 2055, what can we hope for, and what should we aspire to achieve? What will be expected of individuals for them to be considered responsible members of society and to have earned the rights as citizens of what is likely to span multiple bodies in our solar system? Certainly, more will be expected than knowing reading, writing, and arithmetic, passing a driver's test, and being able to find a job and a basic living wage. It seems reasonable that a young adult in 2055, with the help of a cognitive assistant, could have the ability and the experience to rapidly rebuild societal infrastructure from scratch. The ability to understand the world, to work from raw materials, and to achieve the level of 3D printers that can build personal assistants equipped with the sum of societal knowledge in a direct path—this would be a test worthy of 2055 citizenry.

Knowledge has been defined as the ability to channel energy for a purpose (Simms 1971). Technologies and organizations are two proven knowledge amplifiers used to channel energy to achieve purposes beyond the scale of individual human capabilities (Norman 1993). Purpose and capability co-evolve in the accelerating design loops of socio-technical system narratives (Kline 1995). To date, as far as we know, only a single service-oriented species has evolved such socio-technical system narratives that can be passed from generation to generation in written form, and that foresee the transformation and/or demise of that species (Deacon 1998). For *Homo sapiens*, the number of such narratives is growing by the day.

For example, consider the narrative in Superintelligence (Bostrom 2014). To over-simplify this thoughtful book, regarding the co-evolution of purpose and capabilities, the question becomes, how could we choose without locking in forever the prejudices and preconceptions of the present generation? And so, in the narrative about the race between education and catastrophe, capabilities co-evolve with purpose (rights, responsibility, ethics, etc.). Service science is the emerging transdiscipline that studies the evolving ecology of nested, networked service system entities, their capabilities, constraints, rights, and responsibilities. Bostrom states:

> Some intelligent systems consist of intelligent parts
> that are themselves capable of agency. Firms and states

exemplify this in the human world: whilst largely com-
posed of humans they can, for some purposes, be viewed
as autonomous agents in their own right. The motivations of such composite systems depend not only on the
motivations of their constituent sub-agents but also on
how those subagents are organized.... Institutional design is perhaps most plausible in context where it would
be combined with augmentation. If we could start with
agents that are already suitably motivated or that have
human-like motivations, institutional arrangements
could be used as an extra safeguard to increase the chanc-
es the system will stay on course.

What might all this mean for innovation for jobs? Innovation for
jobs is not simply the design of roles that need to be filled in business and society. Furthermore, innovation for jobs is not simply
about designs that match unique individual personal capabilities
with unique individual needs. Innovation for jobs is ultimately
about the design of those institutions (e.g., families, universities,
businesses, and city, state, and national governments) and the
design of augmented individuals and teams within those institutions. Individual capabilities and purpose are shaped by the
larger context of collective capabilities and purposes—our institutions. Throughout most of human history, the family or extended clan provided the institutional arrangements, and jobs for pay
were unnecessary. Only in the last 200 years have businesses and
governments employed large numbers of people in specific job
roles for pay.

Are there an enduring purpose and institutional arrangement that
make sense in a service-oriented world of accelerating knowledge
creation, a world in which the rapidly expanding capabilities of
augmented individuals can reach the point of being dangerous
for the survival of many others, if not the species, if those capabilities are misused? Sen (2001) refers to development as freedom,
but freedom in the context of institutions that ensure responsible
use of capabilities.

Perhaps it is irresponsible to use a capability that one cannot rapidly rebuild from scratch. Education is the institution that provides a rite of passage into today's service-oriented world, and perhaps the purpose of education in the future will be to ensure that individuals can rapidly rebuild knowledge and societal infrastructure from scratch. This is not simply learning about, but learning to do, or, more properly, learning to redo.

If properly redesigned, a new educational institution might provide the basis for a more thorough and lasting examination of human capabilities, constraints, rights, and responsibilities (Proenneke 2009). What if people were only entitled to use capabilities they earned by proving they could rapidly rebuild them from scratch? Would this make people more responsible co-creators of value in a service-oriented world of abundant knowledge and capabilities? If specialization of capabilities (division of labor) is the ultimate goal driving the wealth of nations, where are all the scribes? Clearly, the design of individual and institutional purpose is not simply to specialize capabilities and gain easy, low-cost access to everything. Service science studies the evolution of entities with capabilities, constraints, rights, and responsibilities, and within twenty years cognitive assistants are likely to be an essential element of human performance.

Without the help of cognitive assistants, this responsibility would be too great for most individuals to bear alone. However, with cognitive assistants much more is possible, both in terms of capabilities and responsibilities. Cognitive assistants have the potential to help all of us become more human humans (Christian 2011). Rethinking institutions when all individuals have cognitive assistants is an opportunity that will shape the service-oriented world of 2055.

References

Ackoff, R. L. 1971. Towards a system of systems concepts. *Management Science* 17 (11): 661–671.

Arthur, W. B. 2009. *The nature of technology: What it is and how it evolves*. New York: Simon and Schuster.

Bastiat, F. 1850/1979. *Economic harmonies: The foundations of economics education*. Irvington-on-Hudson, NY.

Bostrom, N. 2014. *Superintelligence: Paths, dangers, strategies*. UK: Oxford University Press.

Brynjolfsson, E., and McAfee, A. 2014. *The second machine age: Work, progress, and prosperity in a time of brilliant technologies*. New York: WW Norton and Company.

Carlson, C. 2015. Computers that love us. URL 20150704: http://www.practiceofinnovation.com/computers-that-love-us/.

Christian, B. 2011. *The most human: What talking with computers teaches us about what it means to be alive*. New York: Anchor.

CSIG 2015. Cognitive Systems Institute Group. URL 20140721 https://www.linkedin.com/groups/Cognitive-Systems-Institute-6729452.

Deacon, T. W. 1998. *The symbolic species: The co-evolution of language and the brain*. New York: WW Norton and Company.

Dire Straits 1985. Money for nothing. URL 20150706: http://www.azlyrics.com/lyrics/direstraits/moneyfornothing.html.

Dobbs, R., Madgavkar, A., Barton, D., Labaye, E., Manyika, J., Roxburgh, C., Lund, S., Madhav, S. 2012. The world at work: Jobs, pay, and skills for 3.5 billion people. McKinsey Global Institute.

Engelbart, D. C. 1962. Augmenting Human Intellect: A Conceptual Framework. SRI Summary Report AFOSR-3223. Doug Engelbart Institute.

Fine, C. H. 1998. *Clockspeed: Winning industry control in the age of temporary advantage*. New York: Basic Books.

Galambos, A. J. 1998. *Sic itur ad astra: The theory of volition (Volume 1)*. San Diego, California: The Universal Scientific Publications Company.

Gershuny, J. 2000. *Changing times: Work and leisure in postindustrial society*. UK: Oxford University Press.

HAT 2015. Hub of All Things. URL 20150721 http://hubofallthings.com/.

Jones, B. F. 2009. The burden of knowledge and the "death of the renaissance man:" Is innovation getting harder? *The Review of Economic Studies* 76 (1): 283–317.

Kan, M. 2015. Foxconn expects robots to take over more factory work. URL 20150707: http://www.pcworld.com/article/2890032/foxconn-expects-robots-to-take-over-more-factory-work.html.

Kline, S. J. 1995. *Conceptual foundations for multidisciplinary thinking*. Palo Alto, CA: Stanford University Press.

Levy, F., and Murnane, R. J. 2012. *The new division of labor: How computers are creating the next job market*. Princeton, NJ: Princeton University Press.

Lusch, R. F., and Vargo, S. L. 2014. *Service-dominant logic: Premises, perspectives, possibilities*. UK: Cambridge University Press.

March, J. G. 1991. Exploration and exploitation in organizational learning. *Organization Science* 2 (1): 71–87.

Mason, P. 2015. The end of capitalism has begun. *The Guardian*. URL 20150719: http://www.theguardian.com/books/2015/jul/17/postcapitalism-end-of-capitalism-begun.

Newell, A., and Simon, H. A. 1976. Computer science as empirical inquiry: Symbols and search. *Communications of the ACM* 19 (3): 113–126.

Norman, D. A. 1993. *Things that make us smart: Defending human attributes in the age of the machine*. New York: Basic Books.

Nordfors, D. 2014. How to disrupt unemployment. *Huffington Post*. URL 20140724: http://www.huffingtonpost.com/david-nordfors/how-innovation-can-disrup-unemployment_b_5616562.html.

NSF 2014. Partnership for innovation: Building innovation capacity (PFI:BIC). Program Solicitation 14-610. National Science Foundation. URL 20150720 http://www.nsf.gov/pubs/2014/nsf14610/nsf14610.htm.

Proenneke, D. 2009. Alone in the wilderness. Bob Swerer Productions. URL 20150720 https://www.youtube.com/watch?v=iYJKd0rkKss.

Pine, B. J., II, and Gilmore, J. H. 1999. *The experience economy: Work is theatre and every business a stage*. Cambridge, MA: Harvard Business Press.

Ricardo, D. 1971. *On the principles of political economy and taxation* (Vol. 165). R. M. Hartwell (ed.). Middlesex: Penguin Books.

Rolling Stones. 1968. The Salt of the Earth. URL 20150711: https://www.youtube.com/watch?v=_DE7w_HSqUU.

Sen, A. 2001. *Development as freedom*. UK: Oxford University Press.

Simms J. R. 1971. *A Measure of Knowledge*. New York: Philosophical Library.

Smith, A. 1991. *The wealth of nations* (Vol. 3). A. S. Skinner (dd.). New York: Prometheus Books.

Spohrer, J. C., and Maglio, P. P. 2010. Toward a science of service systems. In *Handbook of service science* (pp. 157–194). New York: Springer.

Spohrer, J., Golinelli, G. M., Piciocchi, P., and Bassano, C. 2010. An integrated SS-VSA analysis of changing job roles. *Service Science* 2 (1-2): 1–20.

Spohrer, J., Piciocchi, P., and Bassano, C. 2012. Three frameworks for service research: exploring multilevel governance in nested, networked systems. *Service Science* 4 (2): 147–160.

Spohrer, J., Giuiusa, A., and Demirkan, H., Ing, D. 2013. Service science: reframing progress with universities. *Systems Research and Behavioral Science* 30 (5): 561–569.

Spohrer, J., Kwan, S. K., and Fisk, R. P. 2014. Marketing: A service science and arts perspective. In *Handbook of service marketing research*, Rust, R. T. and Huang, M. H., (eds.). Cheltenham, UK: Edward Elgar.

Spohrer, J. 2015 Welcome to IBM Research - Almaden. San Jose, CA. http://www.slideshare.net/spohrer/welcome-to-almaden-20150716-v19.

Spohrer, J., and Banavar, G. 2015 (submitted). Cognition as a service. *AI Magazine*.

Wadhwa, V. 2015. Sorry, but the jobless future isn't a Luddite fallacy. URL 20150707: http://wadhwa.com/2015/07/07/sorry-but-the-jobless-future-isnt-a-luddite-fallacy/.

Wright, R. 2000. Non-zero: The logic of human destiny. New York: Vintage/Random House.

CHAPTER 10

Creative Learning and the Future of Work

By J. Philipp Schmidt, Mitchel Resnick, and Joi Ito[1]

Abstract

The workplace is undergoing a radical transformation. Some jobs are disappearing, as computers and robots take over routine tasks (and even some non-routine tasks). And the jobs that remain are changing dramatically, as workers must continually adapt to an onslaught of new technologies, new sources of information, and new communication channels. Success in the future—for individuals, for companies, for communities, and even for countries as a whole—will depend on the ability to come up with innovative solutions to new and unexpected problems. In short, people must learn to think and to act creatively.

But there is a problem. Today's education systems are not designed to help people develop as creative thinkers. Many of today's schools were originally set up to produce workers for industrial-age factories, and they have not adapted with the times. In too many schools, students are trained to do the type of work that is increasingly being replaced by computers and robots. Instead, we need to help students develop the creative-thinking skills that

---

1   J. Philipp Schmidt is director of Learning Innovation at the MIT Media Lab; cofounder a of Peer 2 Peer University (P2PU)
Mitchel Resnick, LEGO Papert professor of Learning Research and head of the Lifelong Kindergarten group at the MIT Media Lab.
Joichi "Joi" is director of the MIT Media Lab and sits on the boards of Sony, Knight Foundation, MacArthur Foundation, New York Times, and Mozilla.

are needed in a rapidly changing workplace, preparing them for jobs that will be enhanced, not replaced, by new technologies.

In this short article, we propose an alternative vision of learning, drawing on our experiences at the MIT Media Lab. We discuss how the Media Lab's creative and antidisciplinary approach to learning helps prepare students to think creatively, to reason systematically, to work collaboratively, and to learn continuously— precisely the skills that will be needed for success in future work environments. And we argue that today's education systems should be redesigned to enable more people to learn in this way.

The Future of Work

As digital technologies continue to become faster and cheaper, and the fields of artificial intelligence (AI) and machine learning continue to advance, machines are starting to excel at a broader range of tasks and to outperform humans in many ways—particularly at tasks that involve massive amounts of data, speed, accuracy, repetition, reliability, obedience, and computation. The result: machines are starting to take over certain jobs that were traditionally filled by humans.

Increasingly, creativity and ingenuity are becoming the crucial "comparative advantage" for people. As the speed of scientific discovery and technology development continue to accelerate, people will be confronted with more information and more uncertain situations than ever before. How they respond to these situations will depend on their ability to think and work creatively—that is, their ability to come up with their own ways of dealing with new and unexpected situations. Creativity will be relevant not only in high-wage jobs. Empowering people in low-wage jobs, by giving them more agency to come up with creative improvements to their work, will make work more interesting for them and contribute to efficiency and productivity.

Our MIT colleague David Autor argues that the increased use of technology has had a polarizing effect on the labor market. There are more job opportunities in low-education/low-wage and high-education/high-wage jobs, but there are fewer traditional middle-skill jobs (Autor 2014).

The types of low-wage jobs that will not be replaced by machines are those that require high-levels of situational adaptability, personal interactions, and complex motor skills applied creatively. For example, restaurant waiters are constantly faced with new situations or unexpected demands from customers, and hairdressers require a high level of manual dexterity and creativity that are not easily provided by an algorithm. Humans are better than machines at operating in environments like these.

At the other end of the spectrum, high-wage jobs that require complex problem-solving, analysis, and design skills will be filled by people who are able to employ technology in highly creative and productive ways—for example, data scientists who use sophisticated statistical technologies in creative, new ways to play with data in order to identify more efficient ways of producing goods. As Autor points out, the conversation is focused too much on machines replacing humans, and not enough on jobs that benefit from a combination of machines and humans. This is particularly true for high-skill jobs, but also applies to many middle-skill positions.

Middle-skill jobs are most at risk of being replaced by machines, but we might also see the emergence of new types of middle-skill jobs in which humans and machines collaborate in more deeply connected ways than was possible even a few years ago. For example, nurse practitioners might be able to take over more of the tasks of diagnosing and prescribing from doctors by combining their human strengths with expertise from AI-enhanced computer systems. AI systems could sort through vast amounts of information and detect patterns of symptoms that suggest a patient might have a serious condition. By using their own common-sense sensibilities and empathetic understanding of patients, in collaboration with AI systems, nurse practitioners would be better able to give advice and to decide when to escalate patients to a doctor or hospital. In this example, the nurse practitioner is not just a user of the AI system but also could contribute ideas to its design, including how to improve the experience for patients, helping refine the way humans and machines interact.

All three categories of future jobs rely on human abilities that are hard for machines to replace. For workers to move up to higher-wage jobs, creativity and ingenuity will become ever more important—in particular, for unlocking the benefits of powerful complementary machines. Opportunities to apply creativity in low-wage jobs may be more limited, but even here, creating space for workers to make creative adjustments to how their jobs are done not only will make jobs more meaningful but also will make workers more productive. And new types of middle-wage jobs will place greater emphasis on the creative use of technology, and the ability for humans and machines to learn to work together.

There are still many questions about the future of work, but one thing is very clear: developing a narrow set of skills or specific content knowledge will be less relevant for any type of job in the future. Yet, that is exactly what most education systems focus on today.

Today's Education Systems are Rooted in the Past

It is ironic (and distressing) that at the same time that machines are increasingly taking over workplace tasks that don't require any uniquely human abilities, our education systems continue to push children to think and to act like machines. This approach to education became entrenched during the Industrial Revolution, when there was an increasing need for workers who were predictable and punctual, and could accurately perform repetitive tasks. Education systems evolved to the demand of the market and became factories for people who would work in factories, converting playful, creative, and unique human beings into workers who were expected to function more like machines.

One byproduct of the factory model of education is an emphasis on standardized testing to assess the performance of students, teachers, and schools. Standardized testing fit naturally in an industrial-era school system that focused on the delivery of instruction and the management of students. But standardized testing is at odds with the new need to spur curiosity and to foster creativity among learners. We can most easily measure and track the types of routinized skills and knowledge that were needed in industrial-era jobs—and are increasingly being handled by machines. Instead, we need to stop training students for exams that a computer could pass, and instead prepare them to do the type of creative work that robots and machines won't be good at.

Learning over Education

The MIT Media Lab is an experimental testbed for the way technology will shape how we live, work, play, and learn. At any given time, our academic program includes about 150 master's and PhD students who are developing tools and technologies for a better future. These students work on specific research projects that lead to graduate degrees. But more important, the Media Lab aims to prepare the students to thrive in a future that we cannot fully anticipate today—a future in which the ability to use advanced technology creatively will be a crucial skill.

At the core of the Media Lab experience is a focus on learning rather than on education. The difference may seem subtle, but it is important. Media Lab Director Joi Ito, a three-time college dropout, whose job now includes convincing graduate students to stay in school, describes it this way: "Learning is something you do for yourself, and education is something that feels like it is being done to you." This is not to say that there is not a lot of learning that takes place in the education system. Teachers can play a crucial role in fostering, encouraging, guiding, and supporting learning. But too often, schools focus on delivering information and instruction, rather than on helping students develop as curious, creative, lifelong learners.

Since its founding in 1985, the Media Lab has taken a learner-centric approach in its academic and research programs. Media Lab students spend little time in classrooms listening to lectures from faculty members. Rather, they are constantly working on projects and learning through a process of designing, creating, experimenting, and exploring. This approach is based on the constructionist learning theories of Seymour Papert, one of the founding faculty members of the Media Lab. In his research, Papert applied his constructionist ideas to new computer technologies, arguing that computers would be most transformative in children's lives not by delivering information and instruction, but rather by providing them with new opportunities to design, to create, and to express themselves (Papert, 1980). Papert's ideas remain foundational to the Media Lab's research and learning culture today.

Below, we discuss two core elements of the Media Lab's learning approach: creative learning and antidisciplinary research. We believe that these ideas have helped the Media Lab earn its reputation as one of the world's most innovative research labs, and, at the same time, also have helped prepare Media Lab students to thrive in the workplace of tomorrow, where they will need to adapt constantly to ever-changing needs and challenges. Although we developed these ideas in the context of the Media Lab, we believe that they can serve as guiding principles for the design of schools, universities, and other learning organizations.

Creative Learning

Extending the work started by Seymour Papert, researchers in the Media Lab's Lifelong Kindergarten group (led by Mitchel Resnick) have identified four components of a creative learning experience, which we refer to as the four Ps of creative learning: projects, peers, passion, and play (Resnick, 2014). We use these four Ps as guiding principles for the way we design learning environments and experiences, both for our students at the Media Lab and in our outreach efforts beyond the Lab. Indeed, each of the four Ps is essential:

- **Projects**—We learn best when we are actively working on projects—generating new ideas, designing prototypes, making improvements, and creating final products. In the course of working on projects, we learn to improvise, to adapt, to debug, and to iterate. By reflecting on the process of design and iteration, we learn not only to solve specific problems but also to hone our abilities to understand and to design solutions to any problem.

- **Peers**—Learning flourishes as a social activity, with people sharing ideas, collaborating on projects, and building on one another's work. The hardest problems cannot be solved by one person alone, and in our professional lives, we rarely work in isolation. That's why the ability to engage others in our work and to collaborate with them constructively is so important. Sharing ideas with others, and helping them learn, is a great way to deepen our own understanding, because it requires us to explain empathically what we know.

- **Passion**—When we focus on things we care about, we are likely to work longer and harder, to persist in the face of challenges, and to learn more in the process. Research studies have shown that people make their most creative contributions when they are following their passions, not when they are motivated by external rewards. Rewards and pressure can squash, rather than foster, creative thinking. The educational challenge is to help students identify their passions and then to provide them with the support they need to turn their ideas into realities.

- **Play**—Learning involves playful experimentation—trying new things, tinkering with materials, testing boundaries, taking risks, iterating again and again. Play teaches us how to fail early and often, and how to learn from our failures. These skills are critical for entrepreneurs—or anyone who wants to innovate. We need to recognize that different people play and learn in different ways, and we need to provide them with the space and time they need for exploring their own paths.

The four Ps not only shape the learning culture at the Media Lab but also inform the goals and design of our learning research. For example, the four Ps have inspired the design of a variety of initiatives: Read Out Loud, a learning tool for adults with very low literacy; Wildflower, a network of store-front schools that translate Montessori methods for the twenty-first century; and Scratch, a programming environment and online community that enables young people to express themselves creatively and to develop computational fluencies in the process. The four Ps could equally be applied to the design of new types of workplaces, credential systems, or corporate learning experiences.

Antidisciplinary Research

The creative jobs of the future will not fit into boxes as neatly labeled and divided as the professions of today. The positions that involve mastery and the use of powerful technologies will be filled by people who combine a range of different skills from different disciplines. These jobs will require not just interdisciplinary but antidisciplinary thinking and doing.

An interdisciplinary approach seeks to bring different disciplines together; for example, when researchers from different departments collaborate, or ideas from different research groups are combined. But antidisciplinary work isn't the sum of a bunch of disciplines; it is something entirely new. What it means to us is someone or something that defines a new and unique approach rather than fitting within a traditional academic discipline that has its own particular language, frameworks, and methods.

This is a problem for traditional education systems, because today's schools and colleges are set up for clearly separated domain-specific instruction. Throughout much of formal education, courses are arranged by subject and neatly stacked in linear progressions of increasing difficulty. Calculus follows pre-calculus, which follows algebra, which follows pre-algebra.

Moving into higher education, further specialization is not just suggested but required. In most fields, top researchers need deep expertise in narrow micro-disciplines. The call for interdisciplinary work rings hollow when promotion and tenure are based on publications in highly specialized journals. And even if academic programs tried to articulate new combinations of interdisciplinary skills, the patterns of competencies required for the jobs of the future are likely to change much faster than new degree programs could be designed to develop them.

Promoting antidisciplinary learning and research requires unconventional approaches. The kind of scholars we are looking for at the Media Lab are people who don't fit into existing disciplines, because they are either between or simply beyond disciplines. To attract and to find them, we create new positions, such as the "Professor of Other," or we arrange our faculty searches around major issues, such as climate change, rather than around disciplines. Another strategy is to maintain high expectations, but to create much lower barriers to entry. It might seem counter-intuitive, but to be eligible for graduate study at the Media Lab, students need no previous degrees or standardized test scores whatsoever. What we look for instead are interesting projects, surprising combinations of interests, and a curiosity for things that require new connections.

Future work environments will require more designers, thinkers, and innovators with antidisciplinary mindsets. Recruiting, supporting, and nurturing them requires a departure from the silos of our current education systems.

Learning to Shape the Future of Work

The future of work will force us to ask hard questions about the social fabric of our global society. How will we distribute the profits from highly productive labor, when a small number of skilled people with a billion robots can produce most of the things the rest of us need? How will we, as a society, deal with the inequities that result as great wealth accumulates in the hands of a few?

There are a wide range of possible outcomes. At one extreme is a utopian vision in which everyone has access to the things they need, with plentiful leisure time to pursue their interests. At the other extreme is a dystopian vision in which most people toil in low-income jobs that don't require significant cognitive or creative abilities, envious of the opportunities that are open to only a tiny elite.

These are knotty questions, and we believe that the path to answering them requires us to step outside the boundaries of traditional disciplines. We need to redesign the education systems of today, engaging all learners in antidisciplinary and creative learning experiences, and equipping them to shape the work environment of tomorrow and to thrive in it. At the heart of any long-term strategy to prepare people for the jobs they will want to occupy in the future, we need to have a much more intentional approach to support creative learning and antidisciplinary research throughout our education systems.

References

Autor, David H. 2014. Polanyi's paradox and the shape of employment growth. National Bureau of Economic Research Working Paper No. 20485, September 2014. http://www.nber.org/papers/w20485.

Papert, Seymour. 1980. *Mindstorms: Children, computers, and powerful ideas*. New York: Basic Books.

Resnick, Mitchel. 2014. Give P's a chance: Projects, peers, passion, play. Constructionism and Creativity Conference 2014. Vienna, Austria. http://web.media.mit.edu/~mres/papers/constructionism-2014.pdf.

CHAPTER 11
Can the Health Industry Cure the Ailing Job Market?

By Joon Yun[1]

The Labor Shortage Crisis

The twenty-first century is poised to be the health century. The growing demand for health among consumers has the potential to fuel significant job creation. For the health industry, the job crisis that looms ahead is a shortage of *labor*, not jobs.

In the health care industry, as in other industries, technology, innovation, and automation have replaced many functions previously performed by humans, yet job growth in health care continues to exceed job losses. According to the Bureau of Labor Statistics (BLS), between 2002 and 2012 health care experienced the largest annual growth rate (2.3 percent) of jobs among all major industries.[2]

Looking ahead, the BLS estimates that health care jobs will grow at an even higher annualized rate of 2.6 percent between 2012 and 2022.[3] Cumulatively, that means that more than 8 million jobs will be added between 2002 and 2022. To put that number into perspective, the total number of unemployed Americans in 2015 is

---

1 Dr. Joon Yun is managing partner and president of Palo Alto Investors, an investment management firm founded in 1989 with over $1 billion in assets invested in health care.
2 Bureau of Labor Statistics, "Employment Projections – Employment by Major Industry Sector," http://www.bls.gov/emp/ep_table_201.htm.
3 Ibid.

8.6 million, according to the BLS.[4] Thus, the growth in health care jobs will be of a scale that could help offset unemployment issues and job losses elsewhere in the economy.

Even accounting for the expected expansion of health care jobs, many health professions, such as registered nurses, pharmacists, and physicians, are facing increasing labor shortages over the next decade.[5] The aging population, and the associated acceleration of demand for health care, is a major factor in the worsening labor shortage. The situation with physicians is exemplary. Gone are the times when physician shortages mostly involved primary care doctors or rural geographies. Now, shortages of all doctors, including specialists, are expected in cities as well as in rural areas.[6] The expected physician shortage is particularly relevant to the job discussion, because each physician job creates fourteen jobs for staff and related professionals, according to a study by the American Medical Association.[7]

Understaffing is already so pervasive across the health system that, more than in any other industry, consumers are accustomed to expecting delays in service. The waiting room of a health care facility is a cultural institution unto itself, with formidable collections of reading materials to occupy frustrated customers. The understaffing is not without costs. Patient presentations to hospitals outside of the peak staffing hours of 9 a.m. to 5 p.m. on weekdays have long been known to be associated with higher mortality

---

4   Bureau of Labor Statistics, "Economic News Release - Table A-14. Unemployed Persons by Industry and Class of Worker, Not Seasonally Adjusted," http://www.bls.gov/news.release/empsit.t14.htm.

5   American Association of Colleges of Nursing, "Nursing Shortage" http://www.aacn.nche.edu/media-relations/fact-sheets/nursing-shortage; American Association of Colleges of Pharmacy, "Job Outlook for Pharmacists," http://www.aacp.org/resources/student/pharmacyforyou/Pages/joboutlook.aspx; Association of American Medical Colleges, "Physician Shortages to Worsen Without Increases in Residency Training," https://www.aamc.org/download/150584/data/physician_shortages_factsheet.pdf.

6   Association of American Medical Colleges, "Physician Shortages to Worsen Without Increases in Residency Training," https://www.aamc.org/download/150584/data/physician_shortages_factsheet.pdf.

7   American Medical Association, "Physicians Boost the Economy," http://www.ama-assn.org/ama/pub/advocacy/state-advocacy-arc/economic-impact-study.page.

rates, but these gaps of coverage remain an accepted part of the norm in a system stretched thin.[8]

Given the current staffing shortages and the expected increase in shortages anticipated in the future, the growth of health industry jobs predicted by the Bureau of Labor Statistics over the next decade *understates* the industry's job creation potential.

However, tapping into this potential will require addressing the training bottlenecks that plague the health industry. Health professionals, such as physicians, are part of guild systems that have been conservative in expanding their membership. That is beginning to change. Under the directive of the American Association of Medical Colleges (AAMC), medical school spots are on pace to increase 30 percent from 2006 to 2017.[9] While that is good news, record numbers of medical school applicants are nonetheless being turned away, despite the worsening labor shortage.[10]

I am convinced that technology can expand capacity at medical schools without compromising the quality of trainees, at least for the first two years of their training, when learning occurs in lecture halls. The emergence of online learning platforms renders moot the theoretical limit on class size, and the first two years of medical education could potentially be delivered to all prospective doctors at negligible cost. Furthermore, the quality of lectures could be standardized at the highest level through online platforms.

Online platforms, however, cannot resolve the training bottlenecks of the final two years of medical school, when students

8 National Center for Biotechnology Information (PubMed abstracts), "Emergency medical admissions, deaths at weekends and public holiday effect," http://www.ncbi.nlm.nih.gov/pubmed/23345314; "Time of Birth and the Risk of Neonatal Death," http://www.ncbi.nlm.nih.gov/pubmed/16055587; "Increased Mortality Associated with After-hours and Weekend Admission to the Intensive Care Unit: A Retrospective Analysis," http://www.ncbi.nlm.nih.gov/pubmed/21426282.

9 Association of American Medical Colleges, "Medical School Enrollment on Pace to Reach 30 Percent Increase by 2030," https://www.aamc.org/newsroom/newsreleases/335244/050213.html.

10 Association of American Medical Colleges, "Myths and Facts: The Physician Shortage," https://www.aamc.org/download/386378/data/07252014.pdf.

learn as apprentices under the direct supervision of mentors. And online platforms cannot resolve similar training bottlenecks in residency slots, which also are in short supply.[11]

The prevailing wisdom views medical school students and residents as costs to the host institution, presumably on a declining scale as the mentees advance.[12] The clinical training of medical school students is expected to be offset by tuition. The training costs of residents are partially offset by graduate medical education (GME) support from Medicare. AAMC believes that the limit on funding from Medicare is a major bottleneck in medical training,

However, some question whether mentees currently represent a cost or a profit center without GME support for sponsoring institutions.[13] The question revolves around whether medical trainees could more than pay for themselves through increased overall clinical production at below-market wages.[14] Specifically, innovations that increase efficiencies associated with clinical mentorships, so that they become profit centers for sponsoring institutions, could lead to the significant expansion of residency slots. For example:

- Historically, the rate-limiting step in case-based learning for residents in clinical rounds was the intermittent availability of mentor attendings, which could keep the entire resident team idle for most of the day. Going forward, residents will have access to high-quality, case-based learning opportunities

---

11 Ibid.
12 Association of American Medical Colleges, "What Does Medicare Have to Do with Graduate Medical Education?" https://www.aamc.org/advocacy/campaigns_and_coalitions/gmefunding/factsheets/253372/medicare-gme.html.
13 Wynn, Barbara O., Smalley, Robert, and Cordasco, Kristina M., "Does It Cost More to Train Residents or to Replace Them? A Look at the Costs and Benefits of Operating Graduate Medical Education Programs," Rand Corporation, http://www.rand.org/content/dam/rand/pubs/research_reports/RR300/RR324/RAND_RR324.pdf.
14 Rampell, Catherine, "Solving the Shortage in Primary Care Doctors," New York Times, December 14, 2013, http://www.nytimes.com/2013/12/15/business/solving-the-shortage-in-primary-care-doctors.html.

from leading mentors on the Internet and will explore cases with students at other institutions.

- Advanced clinical training on leading edge devices, such as robotic surgery devices, has been difficult and expensive to provide for young trainees. The costs could be reduced significantly through simulation technologies made possible by the advent of virtual reality platforms.

- Countersigning preliminary orders of residents by attending physicians, which still largely occurs today as a pen-to-paper process, can lead to substantial delays in treatment to patients and higher costs to health educational institutions. Wider deployment of mobile technologies, such as electronic countersigning, in training institutions can mitigate communication inefficiencies, speed workflow, improve outcomes, and reduce the overall cost of training the next generation physicians.

In addition to cost constraints, another major bottleneck in medical schools and residency spots is the paucity of mentor-physicians to supervise students and junior staff. The current shortage of doctors is a potential cause of the future shortage of doctors. Thus, increasing physician-workers will be a feed-forward force expanding the future pool of physicians.

As the delivery of health care service improves with the expansion of the health care workforce, human longevity will continue to improve. Unless the diseases of aging are cured, the increase in longevity will further increase future health care consumption in a virtuous cycle. Thus, the health care job engine is one that can create more jobs as more people enter the industry. That is the kind of positive dynamic that can catalyze an employment revolution.

CHAPTER 12

Creative Learning

By Esther Wojcicki[1]

Abstract

Moonshots in Education is a blended learning style for the classroom that has been successfully applied and developed over three decades. The more a teacher does for the student and the more control the teacher has over that student, the less creativity and innovation evolve and the less genuine learning of essential twenty-first century working skills takes place. The traditional top-down methods for education put the teacher and the system in control, and the student has little or no interest in the learning. Kids may learn many facts but don't necessarily transfer them to the real world. They want to get the answer right, and so they avoid risk and learn to fear failure. But these problems do not appear when students are collaborators and the teacher is a coach or an advisor. The key to success is to put kids in control in the classroom, while maintaining five important components that can be expressed by the acronym TRICK: trust, respect, independence, collaboration, and kindness. It is a real-world program in which students receive the trust and respect they crave and know that their work will be read by thousands of people. No matter what the situation is, they need the communication skills known as the four Cs: critical thinking, communication, collaboration,

---

1   Esther Wojcicki is founder of Palo Alto High School Media Arts Program and
     vice chair of Creative Commons.

and creativity. The students in the program have used the tools they acquired to succeed in a variety of professions, ranging from actors, doctors, lawyers, yoga instructors, entrepreneurs, teachers, and more.

Empowering Students

My goal is to help teachers work less, be more effective, and empower kids. My methods are based on thirty-one years in the classroom. I realized early that the more a teacher does for the student and the more control the teacher has over that student, the less creativity and innovation evolve and the less genuine learning happens. One problem with a top-down system for education today is that the teacher and the system are in control and the student has little or no interest in the learning. Kids may learn many facts but don't necessarily transfer them to the real world. This lack of transfer is one of the major problems. Students want to get the answer right and will do whatever it takes, but in doing this they avoid risk and learn to fear failure.

My parents were impoverished Russian Jewish immigrants. We had no health care, food was limited, and all my clothes were hand-me-downs. We lived in a one-bedroom apartment in East Los Angeles. My father was an artist, and you know how much artists make—nothing. Maybe the adversity made me want to be practical. I think that could have been the motivation.

I was independent from the day I stepped into kindergarten. I always wanted to relate what I was doing to the real world; it was an enduring passion of mine. I remember wondering why my friend would read books about animals, fiction about animals. "You aren't a dog," I thought. I had difficulty reading those books. I was punished often for incorrect "deportment"—talking in class, sharing answers with another student, or, worse, returning late from recess.

I also wanted to help other kids. One reason I was punished often was that I helped other kids with classwork, which was not allowed. I also wanted to help other children make better choices. I will never give in to those who punish kids for collaborating. Helping each other is a life skill; it is not cheating.

I have always been interested in how people learn. I noticed that some of my friends learned quickly and others didn't. I wondered why this was, and my curiosity about this has stayed with me for life.

My own children were my first opportunity to try my educational ideas—my first class. I gave my children much more freedom to be independent than parents do today. I understand why parents want to be in control. The world today seems much more dangerous. Maybe I, like parents of my generation, was just less informed. We hadn't heard about kidnappings and child molestations. Our news sources were newspapers, radio, and television, and news was much slower.

As a mother with a teacher's mindset, I wondered how early my children could learn. I taught Janet to swim at eleven months, Anne at two, and Susan at two and a half years. Anne learned to ice skate at three. Janet taught herself to read at three, watching Sesame Street.

Children are human—they want to be in control, too. I taught mine to help around the house—to feel that they had more control of their environment. Susan was entrusted with babysitting her sisters at five. I was there but she had specific responsibilities. Children are smarter and learn skills far earlier than parents realize.

This empowerment started early. My kids mention what they call "the lemon girl experience." They wanted to earn money to go to the dime store, so, for several years, they sold our lemons to neighbors for five cents each. Susan was six, Janet, five and Anne, three. They earned money and then spent hours at the dime store choosing what they wanted.

Teaching for thirty-one years, I have tried to find the best way to engage students and to teach skills, to reach all my students and make learning relevant to the real world. My earliest guess was that kids who didn't learn weren't less intelligent—they just didn't care.

As a new teacher in the early 1980s at Palo Alto High School, I had a schedule that included journalism and English. The journalism program was small. I had nineteen students in advanced journalism and fifteen in beginning journalism. I was supposed to use a textbook called *Presstime*. It looked okay, superficially. It had chapters on the history of the press, on printing equipment, and on different story types and how to write them. Tellingly, it is no longer available, even on Google Books.

After two months of using *Presstime* and seeing my students lose interest, I found that my curiosity about how to teach most effectively resurfaced. I wondered, how do I excite them about journalism? Throw away the book and maybe get fired? Plow ahead and force the kids to answer the questions at the end of the chapters?

I took the riskier route. I tossed the book and waited to be fired. By December, no one noticed, except the kids, who were happy. I replaced the book with issues of the *Palo Alto Times Tribune*. We read the paper daily and discussed the story types. I wanted to teach all the journalistic styles: news, features, reviews, opinion, and sports. The kids loved it—it made more sense, and the *Tribune* served as a professional model for the newspaper we created, the *Campanile*, named after the campus tower. They learned more, the paper was better, and class enrollment kept growing. I started in 1984, and by 1987 enrollment was up to thirty.

We were producing our newspaper on a Justowriter, a typewriter that justified text. For kids who didn't type, we hired students for a dollar per hour to type for them. Those who could type typed their own stories. After typing the story, students cut them to size with an X-acto knife—unimaginably risky today. I handed out lots of them, saying, "Be careful not to cut yourself or you will bleed on your story, then have to retype it." The next step was waxing the page and pasting it on a layout page on a light table. The goal was to get the stories straight so our paper looked professional.

One day in the fall of 1986, while walking in a Los Altos shopping center, I saw the first Apple Macintosh computer. It could type long documents easily. Corrections were simple. I was intrigued. But it cost five thousand dollars, too much for a teacher, so I wrote a grant application to the state of California asking for seven of those machines. Although I was discouraged from applying by my school's administration, who said I was wasting my time, my grant was awarded, which shocked me and as well as the administration.

The day the computers arrived was exciting. But none of us knew anything about computers. Everyone said, "It's just a phase and won't last." No one knew how to even turn them on. They sat in my classroom for weeks. Then it dawned on me: ask my students what to do.

This was quite an announcement for a teacher in those days, as we teachers tried to think of ourselves as fountains of knowledge. But the kids were thrilled to help *me*, the teacher, do something exciting.

It took weeks to figure out by trial and error how to use the computers and how to network them (what did *networking* mean?). We got a program, PageMaker, from the father of one of my students, who worked at Aldus Corporation. We had to figure out how to reprogram it to save data on the disks. The kids figured it out and at year-end we wrote a report to the state. The project was a success.

This was how a new age of newspaper publishing had been born, at least in my eyes, along with a new way of teaching: collaborative, project-based learning in which I was a coach and the kids learned by discovery.

My life changed, the program changed, and student learning soared. By 1992, we had fifty kids in the class, and I was moved to a lecture center to accommodate all of them. Now I had more computers, which I had to buy with funds I raised in the community. The district still didn't take computers seriously and had no plans to use them.

I never denied a student applicant, though the declared class limit was 28.5 students. The administration thought I was nutty and other faculty members thought I was a maverick, but they let me continue because student and parent demand was so strong.

The newspaper had grown from six to eight pages to twenty pages. I had to include stories from all my students, so the paper expanded. The cost increased, so I organized a business manager and an advertising manager, and the kids had to sell advertising to support the paper. It was tough for them—they had no idea how to sell ads—but I devised a scheme based on what I had read, and it worked. The paper became self-supporting.

By 1998, I had eighty kids in the class—too many—so I started another class, Broadcast Journalism, and pulled out twenty-five kids to form it, running two classes simultaneously. We planned the shows during class, and I had the students do the planning while the newspaper editors and staff led the newspaper program.

This three-ring circus worked. After class, the new broadcast class and I walked a mile to the community-access TV station, Cable Co-op, where we got help on how to use the television equipment. It was exciting, and we soon came out with thirty-minute segments every other week, broadcasting to the Palo Alto area. It was so successful that, in 2000, I hired another teacher for it. Conveniently, Comcast bought Cable Co-op and didn't want the old equipment. They agreed to donate it to Palo Alto High.

As the overall program grew, I started additional publications to take the enrollment pressure off of the newspaper. These included:

- *InFocus*, broadcast journalism, in 2000
- *Verde*, a news magazine and website, in 2000
- *Voice*, web journalism, in 2002

- *Viking*, a sports magazine and website, in 2007
- *C Magazine*, an arts and culture magazine, in 2012
- *Agora*, a foreign affairs magazine, in 2013
- *Proof*, a photo magazine (started by Margo Wixom), in 2014
- Radio journalism (started by Paul Kandell), in 2014

In addition, we continued to publish the newspaper, the *Campanile*, and the yearbook, the *Madrono*, both of which had been started in 1918.

We now have 600 students in all of the programs, including photography and video production. It is the nation's largest media-arts program. In 2014, the school opened a new 25,000-square-foot media arts center to house the entire journalism program. There are now five journalism teachers, and journalism writing is taught in all freshman English classes. The goal is to give students an opportunity to learn new writing skills useful in the social-media age.

The program philosophy is the same as when I started with the Macintosh computers: Students are collaborators, and the teacher is a coach or advisor. I have been teaching a blended learning style long before it was named and recognized as a movement in education.

Building Trust and Respect with TRICK

In February 2015 I published *Moonshots in Education: Launching Blended Learning in the Classroom*. The book's goal was to tell teachers and administrators nationwide and worldwide about the power of giving kids control in the classroom and testing them with trust and respect. There are five important components to my teaching style, summarized in my acronym, TRICK:

- T = Trust
- R = Respect
- I = Independence

- C = Collaboration
- K = Kindness

This is the classroom's secret sauce. No matter how beautiful the building, how many electronic devices, or how great the curriculum, if kids dislike the teacher, no learning will happen. Teaching and learning are all about relationships. The late Rita Pierson gave an inspiring TED talk in 2013 about education in which she said, "James Comer, Professor of Child Psychiatry at Yale, says that no significant learning can occur without a significant relationship. George Washington Carver says all learning is understanding relationships."

Relationships are KEY.

At first I had difficulty getting the administration to accept my pedagogy, especially in the 1980s when I started. Classes were aligned in rows. Kids could talk only when the teacher recognized them. Most class activity was reading, writing, and listening to the teacher. I found that system ineffective, so I changed to more collaboration in my classes—English, math, social studies.

Administrators thought my classes were out of control when they saw kids working collaboratively. Collaboration on homework was considered cheating and students were suspended for it. It was a battle. Some of my early students tell me that I felt alienated from the mainstream. I was convinced that my method worked, so I persevered. I knew that making learning relevant and real-world engaged the kids. I found it especially easy in math, because everyone needs math to live effectively. I taught Algebra I and geometry, and created real-life problems for the kids to solve. I taught math only for two years before going on to teaching language arts.

It wasn't easy being a maverick, but I did it because it worked. The kids were happy, and they learned and wanted to be there. That's why I focus on helping other teachers have classes where students want to be. I know that they're learning. The teacher's life improves, too. If the teacher is happy, the students will be happy to be there.

TRICK in Practice

Here is a description of how each component of TRICK works in practice.

Trust

The first thing to establish in the classroom is a culture of trust. That does not mean the students are free to do what they want; it means that they trust each other to help in the learning process, and the teacher trusts the students. Boundaries must be established early. Teachers can use various exercises and games to build trust.

Since the teacher is in control, he or she must take the initiative to create situations that require students to be trustworthy. Opportunities arise daily. For example, having students work in teams and be responsible to the team teaches trust. Creating a group blog or website gives students a natural way to develop trust in the team. If the teacher trusts the team, it builds a community of trust in the classroom.

The key to building trust is *to actually trust the students*. Counterintuitive? No. It's the only way to effectively build trust. In my advanced journalism class, each student has an individual story assignment, so no two students do the same thing. Some stories about issues in the school, the district, or the city are particularly sensitive. It takes a leap of faith to trust students to get the information right and to write it up objectively. We publish the results online, typically garnering thousands of views, and in hard copy for 3,000 local residents. Students have told me that trusting them to write the stories is significant in building their self-esteem.

The students also publish a newspaper or magazine. Each class has an enrollment of seventy students working in teams on the paper or magazine. Six editors-in-chief manage the class, giving the students critical leadership experience and a sense of control over the publication. The magazine classes have an enrollment of thirty-five and an editorial board of three editors. Each student in each class has a title matching his or her responsibilities—news editor, editorial-page editor, feature-page editor, and so on.

Besides having the students produce publications, I routinely let the students teach. For example, I designate one day a week on which the kids take over the class for an hour. Having kids teach each other regularly, in small groups, also creates trust in the class.

I encourage my students to help with the technology. I use Google Docs to create documents and Adobe software to publish them. New products emerge daily, and although many of them might be useful, I have little time to evaluate them. And so I ask my students to seek potentially useful new software, to learn how to use it, and to share it with the class.

Another way to enhance trust is to give students my home phone number, cell number, and e-mail address and to tell them to contact me when they have problems, but not after a specified evening hour. Giving out that information creates a culture of trust and caring. All students also have the same contact data for all other students, including home phones, cell phones, and email addresses.

I routinely like to laugh at my own mistakes. We all make mistakes and teaching students that mistakes are part of life is an important lesson in helping them accept themselves. The mistakes are easy to find; every day something does not go as planned. Teachers who are willing to show that they're not perfect, don't know everything, and can laugh at themselves can more easily develop trust.

Finally, perhaps most important, I put my students in situations requiring them to think for themselves. They may stumble and have difficulties, but the key is to support them while letting them solve the problem themselves. This builds trust in themselves, in the class as a whole, and between teacher and students.

Respect[2]

Teachers must respect their students, especially in today's world, where class members may come from different backgrounds and experiences. Each student has unique gifts, even if he or she also has unique problems. As a teacher, I know how difficult it can be to respect students who create problems in the classroom, but the teacher must show respect. It helps students feel better about themselves.

Respect is part of trust. I trust my kids and respect them, and, in turn, they trust and respect me. Someone must start the process, and it cannot be the students, since the teacher is in charge.

Independence[3]

We all like independence. For most children, the desire for independence starts at age two—they want to do everything themselves, to their parents' chagrin. In elementary school, students want to be independent, too, but as they progress, they become more dependent on the teacher. By high school—if taught via the old model—they are waiting to be told what to do. But high school is a time when the students' drive for independence should peak. Teachers can encourage this drive by giving students an opportunity to devise their own projects within defined guidelines. For example, students could have a writing assignment in which they

---

2   For resources to help teachers develop respect in the classroom, visit the website of the Association for Supervision and Curriculum Development, a leader in developing and delivering innovative programs that empower educators to support the success of each learner, at www.ascd.org. In particular, see Jonathan Cohen, Richard Cardillo, and Terry Pickeral, "Creating a Climate of Respect," *Educational Leadership* 69, no.1 (September 2011), http://www.ascd.org/publications/educational-leadership/sept11/vol69/num01/Creating-a-Climate-of-Respect.aspx.

3   One obstacle to independence is the challenge in correlating curricula with the Common Core testing requirements; neither the teacher nor the students has much independence in what's studied. But there is independence in how they reach the Common Core goals. To learn more, see Dinah Mack and Holly Epstein Ojalvo, "Independence Day: Developing Self-Directed Learning Projects," *New York Times, The Learning Network* (March 21, 2011), http://learning.blogs.nytimes.com/2011/03/21/independence-day-developing-self-directed-learning-projects/?_php=true&_type=blogs&_r=0.

pick the topic. It could be a restaurant review, with each student reviewing a restaurant of his or her choice.

Collaboration[4]

Collaboration is an important part of the culture of the blended classroom. Students love to work with peers, especially when working on a project they selected. The main attraction of school for most students is peer contact. If teachers make the environment a friendly, collaborative workspace where students feel comfortable, more learning happens.

Kindness

The importance of kindness is self-evident. If students feel that the teacher is kind, they want to learn. I recall many instances of being kind to students who made mistakes. It paid off. The students were grateful, because it made them feel relaxed and accepted. Being kind not only in school, but in life in general, makes the difference. As the American religious leader William J. H. Boetcker put it, "Your greatness is measured by your kindness; your education and intellect by your modesty; your ignorance is betrayed by your suspicions and prejudices, and your real caliber is measured by the consideration and tolerance you have for others."

Examples of Articles Written by Students, and Their Impact

Over the years many impactful articles have been published in the *Campanile*. These articles, usually opinion pieces, editorials, or news, have had a profound impact on the school community.

---

4   To learn more about improving classroom collaboration, see Hans Peter Wachter, "Improving Classroom Learning through Student Collaboration: Learning Outcomes in a LearnLab Teaching Environment," http://www. academia.edu/637980/Improving_classroom_learning_through_student_ collaboration_learning_outcomes_in_a_learnlab_teaching_environment. Also see Patrick Jermann, Amy Soller, and Martin Muelenbrock, "From Mirroring to Guiding: A Review of State of the Art Technology for Supporting Collaborative Learning," from Proceedings of the First European Conference on Computer-Supported Collaborative Learning, http://citeseerx.ist.psu.edu/viewdoc/ summary;jsessionid=CBDE1C045C39019A0401ECCC6E4A463E?doi= 10.1.1.26.2186.

There is nothing like giving teenagers an opportunity to control their learning and their learning environment to engage them. Here are examples of some articles from the Palo Alto High School student press over the past twenty-five years. They represent a tiny portion of the stories that had an impact, but they represent the student voice effectively.

Teacher-Advisor System

One story published in 1990 cited the lack of appropriate academic counseling for students. It sounds mundane, but it started a revolution. Students polled seniors, asking how many had four-year plans that met the requirements for the college of their choice. The results were disturbing: about 40 percent of students had no proper plan. Kids were just randomly selecting courses without knowing whether they met university requirements.

That story resulted in Palo Alto High School's starting a new teacher-advisor counseling program that remains a success today. Under this program, the student body is divided into groups of students who work with a teacher-advisor to ensure that their needs and questions are being addressed. Each teacher who volunteers for the program has about fifty-five students to counsel, far better than previous arrangement in which the four counselors each had a caseload of 500 students.

To summarize: the students ran a poll, collected the data, analyzed it, and then wrote a story. This is real-world experience had an impact. Students feel empowered when they can control their environment, when adults in the community respect their work, and when the school can change to meet their needs.

In many states, students don't receive First Amendment rights. Their work is censored by the principal and the advisor, censorship made possible by the Supreme Court Hazelwood decision. (In January 1988, the Supreme Court handed down its decision in the case *Hazelwood School District v. Kuhlmeier* that upheld the right of public high school administrators to censor stories in student press.)

California is an anti-Hazelwood State and, since 1977, has had a law on its books protecting student expression (California Education Code, No. 48950). Other anti-Hazelwood states include Arkansas, Colorado, Iowa, Kansas, and Massachusetts.

Living Skills Classes

In the early 1990s, the *Campanile* published a story about how the majority of sexually active students were having unprotected sex. This information came from a school poll on student sexual behaviors conducted by student reporters. As a result of the poll and the subsequent outcry, the school established a district-wide program called Living Skills to teach students about issues such as protected sex.

The program's curriculum gives students knowledge and skills that enables them to (1) make informed, responsible decisions about issues affecting personal health and well-being; (2) establish and sustain healthy, rewarding interpersonal relationships; (3) manage life crises, and (4) cultivate the understanding, appreciation, and practice of democratic values and behavior appropriate for a responsible community member.

The program continues today in both Palo Alto high schools, Gunn and Palo Alto High. This type of impact on the community and the school gives students a sense of doing something meaningful.

Rape Culture in High Schools

In 2014, our news magazine *Verde* published an article titled "Rape Culture" about a Palo Alto high school girl who was raped at a local party; the article used that example to discuss a culture prevalent on education campuses nationwide. The article caused public outcry, including an investigation by the Office of Civil

Rights, which was concerned about bullying on campus that allegedly occurred after the rape.

It was hard for the students to research and write that story, but it highlighted a problem on high school and college campuses nationwide. The problem goes beyond Palo Alto High School or even California. The main lesson learned is that a reporter can open the community's eyes but cannot solve the problem alone.

Like all of the other investigative stories our students have written, this story is a real-world problem. Writing about it gives students an opportunity to weigh in on an urgent issue. In general, all the stories in all our publications involve some aspect of the real world, which is one reason why students are so attracted to the program.

Conclusion

Our journalism program is a real-world program in which students receive the trust and respect they crave and know that their work will be read by thousands of people. All classes in all areas of the curriculum should have a project that relates to the real world. I have been advocating for 20 percent time for all classes—that is, give students 20 percent of class time to work on a project with real-world implications. Such subjects must relate to the real world. Tell the students and let them apply the skills they learn in class to the world around them.

The students in the journalism program have gone on to careers in many professions—actors, doctors, lawyers, yoga instructors, entrepreneurs, teachers.

My idea is to give them the tools they need to succeed in whatever career they choose. No matter what the situation is, they need communication skills, the 4 Cs: critical thinking, communication, collaboration, and creativity. They get all these and more in a program that treats students with trust, respect, and kindness, and promotes innovation.

50266458R00119

Made in the USA
Lexington, KY
09 March 2016